Reboot Your Career:

27 Ways to Reinvent Yourself in the Workplace...
(If You Still Have a Job!)

Frederick Fell Publishers, Inc
2131 Hollywood Blvd., Suite 305
Hollywood, Fl 33020
www.Fellpub.com
email: Fellpub@aol.com

Frederick Fell Publishers, Inc
2131 Hollywood Blvd., Suite 305
Hollywood, Fl 33020

For information about special discounts for bulk purchases. Please contact Frederick Fell Special Sales at business@fellpublishers.com.

Designed by Elena Solis

Manufactured in the United States of America

14 13 12 11 10 9 8 7 6 5 4 3 2

Library of Congress Cataloging-in-Publication Data

Fogel, Peter, 1958-
 Reboot your career : 27 ways to reinvent yourself in the workplace : (if you still have a job!) / by Peter Fogel.
    p. cm.
 ISBN 978-0-88391-195-2 (pbk.)
 1. Career development. I. Title.
 HF5381.F64 2011
 650.1--dc22
                        2011005680

ISBN 13: 978-0-88391-195-2

Reboot Your Career:

27 Ways to Reinvent Yourself in the Workplace...
(If You Still Have a Job!)

Peter J. Fogel

Kim,
Thankyou
for reviewing
my Book

Enjoy
[signature]

TABLE OF CONTENTS

DEDICATION

This book is dedicated to Murray, Lilly, Carole, Stan, Roberta, and Judy (and you know why!)

ACKNOWLEDGEMENTS

There are certain people you come across in your passage through life who always have your back, no matter what setbacks you are going through.

It's these folks who believe in you, appreciate your work and contribution, and help pave the way for your success.

To begin, a hearty "I can't wait for my royalty check" appreciation to my publisher, Don Lessne of *Frederick Fell Publishers*, who gave this book a home.

To the folks at *Early to Rise* — and especially Jason, the associate publisher, thank you for allowing my articles to reach a broader audience.

A huge hug for an amazing copywriter and even better friend, Donna Romano Doyle. You put up with me even when I swear my phone call to you will only take "two minutes" of your valuable time. The next thing you know it's a forty-five minute bitch fest where we're both popping antacids.

To Peter Schaible, a superb on-line copywriter and my SEO Guru mentor, thank you for your friendship, support and for helping me reinvent my SEO skills!

To my webmaster and good friend, Mike Sebar of PC Techtime. Thank you for the exceptional work done on my websites and for allowing me to always pay for dinner whenever we get together socially. Always an honor!

To my publicist, Penny C. Sansevieri, President of Author Marketing Experts, thank you for your hard work and for taking *Reboot Your Career* viral.

A grateful thanks to Elena Solis for her creativity in designing the book cover.

Thank you to Donna Eliassen for the outstanding copy editing of my manuscript and to Marta Tanrikulu for the fine indexing done on the book with such short notice. You ladies, rock!

To my favorite chiropractor, Dr. Scott Larit of the *Larit Chiropractic and Wellness Center*. Your firm but gentle adjustments on my lower back are always welcome. I especially appreciate your superior branding message: Healing one patient at a time... as long as your deductible is met!

JUST READ WHAT OTHERS SAY ABOUT "REBOOT YOUR CAREER"...

"This great book shows you a step-by-step program to make yourself valuable getting paid more and promoted faster in any job."
-**Brian Tracy, Author,** *Maximum Achievement*

"Peter Fogel has experienced turbulence and reinvention in his own career. He offers a flight plan for you to reflect on your own career progress and possible mid course corrections. This is a fun read of a very serious topic as you evaluate your self worth and contribution along with what gives you happiness, satisfaction and the opportunity to leave a lasting legacy."
-**Howard Putnam, Former CEO Southwest Airlines, Author,** *The Winds of Turbulence*
www.HowardPutnam.com

"*Reboot Your Career* is an irreverent, highly relevant guide to building a career. With a mix of dead philosophers, pop culture, and Peter Fogel's unique perspective on knowing yourself, branding, and overcoming challenges, you'll leave with actions you can take immediately to change the course of your work life."
-**Jennifer Colosimo, CEO at FranklinCovey Company, and co-author with Stephen R. Covey of** *Great Work, Great Career.*

"With record unemployment, and people worried about holding on to their careers, this book could not be more timely. The Contribution Statement alone is worth ten times the price of the book."
-**Bob Bly, Author of 70 Books, including** *Become A Recognized Authority In Your Field*

"Never before has a book been so relevant for the times than Peter's book, *Reboot Your Career*. If you want to learn how to master the process to reinvent yourself, your brand, and your income potential, devour this book! And believe me, you'll laugh your way through it!"
-**Lisa Jimenez M.Ed., International Speaker and Best-Selling Author of** *Conquer Fear!*
www.Rx-Success.com

"If you haven't reinvented yourself in today's economy, economies of the future will reinvent you. Your choice is not if you will change—it's a matter of when, how, and if it's by your design or not. If you want more out of your career, life, and financial future, you owe it to yourself to not only read this book but devour it and apply it NOW!"
-**Spike Humer Author, Speaker, and Performance-Enhancement Expert**
www.spikehumer.com

"*Reboot Your Career* gives the principles, concepts, and the no-brainer actions you need to put forth if you're truly serious about reinventing yourself. Fogel shows you how to keep your sense of humor through this journey. But just as important, he outlines the steps you need to get results fast! With focus and determination, you can reach your career goals, regardless where you are in the corporate pecking order!"
-Tom McCarthy, Author of *FIRE-UP Your Presentations and Talking to Win*, **Speaker and Peak Performance Coach**
www.tommcarthy.com

"It is a very tough world out there and if you have not taken steps to reinvent or renew yourself you will be unpleasantly surprised. Peter Fogel has written a road map for you to do what you need to do, and most importantly, do it while at the same time having fun and a good time. This book should be a best seller."
-Dr. Joachim de Posada CSP, Author of the best seller *Don't Eat the Marshmallow… Yet: The secret to sweet success in work and life.*

"*Reboot Your Career* gives readers a guide on how to bring out their uniqueness in today's challenging career environment. Peter Fogel inspires you, with his humor and insights, to get out of your comfort zone so you can stretch your talents to the maximum. This book gives you the necessary tools to become indispensable to your boss and company. Once you do that, your sky's the limit into how you can achieve complete career satisfaction."
-Dr. Tony Alessandra, author of *The Platinum Rule, Charisma, and Switched On Selling*

"Peter Fogel has written THE book that is the most important book everyone who has a job must read. Let's face it, today having a job doesn't mean security. This book will give every employee the necessary tools to be valuable to their companies and to create the entrepreneur spirit."
-Terri Levine, The Business Growth Guru, Bestselling Author of *Work Yourself Happy*
www.TerriLevine.com

"*In Reboot Your Career*, author Peter Fogel offers so many ideas, and in many cases, startling perspectives that despite the vicissitudes of the economy, you can't help but find a strategy that will work for you to keep your career progressing."
-Jeff Davidson, MBA, CMC, author of *The 60 Second Innovator*

"The only job security you'll ever have is your own ability. To learn how you can increase your value to your company, read and reread *Reboot Your Career*. It will give you the edge you need to succeed in today's business environment."
-Jim Donovan, author and speaker
www.JimDonovan.com

"In today's marketplace, many people are finding a need to reinvent themselves. If you are one of these people, you will want to read this book. Peter Fogel has given us a treasure map of practical information in an easy-to-read-and-digest humorous style. This is a must read for anyone who needs to restart, jump start, or make a change in his or her present career."
-Judi Moreo, CSP, Author, *You Are More Than Enough*
www.judimoreo.com

"If you have a job then you MUST READ THIS BOOK. In *Reboot Your Career*, author Peter Fogel offers essential tips, tools, and strategies to help expand your career opportunities, reinvent yourself, and get the essential skills required to prosper in the new business environment."
-Lewis Harrison, Success Coach and Speaker, Author of 9 Books
www.RealUGuru.com

"*Reboot Your Career* reveals what most successful entrepreneurs know: that learning how to effectively market and brand yourself will take you further in your career and return you more dividends than you ever thought possible. It doesn't take genius, it doesn't take innate talent. Anyone with drive and focus can reinvent themselves if they put forth the effort. Peter Fogel's book lays it out for you succinctly and in a fun manner. Read it so you can DO it!"
-David Newman, www.doitmarketing.com

"*Reboot Your Career* not only reveals in detail how to find the passion in your career again, but it also lights you a path on how you can contribute to your company on a deeper level. The result? You CAN find fulfillment in your career right where you're at this very moment!"
-Patricia Ball, CSP, CPAE, Past National President of National Speakers Association.

FOREWORD

For close to thirty years, I have either owned, invested, or consulted with over twenty-five companies in a variety of industries. There were start-ups that had revenue of a few million dollars, to my main client today, an information powerhouse that has revenues in excess of 275 million a year.

My goal, during this time in business, was to have only two kinds of employees: Stars and Superstars.

Stars are workers who show up on time, ready to get going, and enthusiastically put in a full day of work for you, always putting your customers' interests first. Superstars have all the good qualities of Stars, but they also possess the rare ability to create corporate growth.

Everyone that is answering your phones, configuring your data, making your products, handling customer problems, and processing and fulfilling orders should be a Star employee.

And everyone who is managing all those Stars should be a Star too. That said, the growth side of any business should be manned by Superstars, for only Superstars are capable of creating and marketing innovative ideas. Not only that, but you need Superstars to create and manage your profits.

Unfortunately, due to an ever changing business environment (expansion overseas, downsizing domestically), you won't find many Stars and Superstars in the job market.

Why? Simply because they are already working happily for other people. Oh, sure, if you're a boss you might be able to poach a few through recruitment companies. However, for the most part, you will have to create your own. Once you do, I can pretty much guarantee you'll have a feeling of real accomplishment.

The secret to creating Stars and Superstars is to hire their untrained and unmotivated counterparts (or first cousins) — *very good and great people!*

Simply put, very good people turn into Stars and great people turn into Superstars. Make no mistake, depending on what stage your company is at, the right employee(s) can make or break you. With so many new people coming on every year, there will surely be a few bad ones.

Nevertheless, just because the chances of having clunkers increase as your payroll grows doesn't mean you have to accept them.

Being a bad employee is not an isolated situation. This behavior is sickening and contagious. Jack Welch is famous for having said that he routinely fires 10% of his work force every year.

I don't know if that is the right approach, because I think it's possible to have a bad employee percentage of less than 10%. That said, I do believe that when you spot a bad employee you should do everything you can to make him good fast. Regrettably, if that fails, you should fire him.

Let's examine the heart and soul of any company, your worker (and future "entrepreneur"). If that is you, then you're probably at a crossroads in your professional life, which is why you picked up this book.

Perhaps you're treading water in your current position and are unsure of your future. (And you should be!)

You want more, whether it is responsibilities, a promotion, work that is more challenging, or the opportunity to make more meaningful contributions to your company. You feel something is missing at your job that can only be identified as "The X factor!" And you won't be content until you get "it".

If that's you, then good for you. That's the first step. The second is to ask yourself some very vital questions about your future.

Where do you see yourself in the next few years? At the same company, or somewhere else, doing the same work? Are you getting the respect for your contributions? Or do your ideas fall on deaf ears?

Most of all, do you see yourself as a future Star or Superstar at your company that will allow you to reach your true potential?

And if you're a boss, are you willing to do what it takes to discover and nurture your next Star or Superstar?

Again, if you said YES, then you, dear reader (whether you are the boss or worker), are quite fortunate to have in your hands *Reboot Your Career*.

Peter Fogel's book is loaded with proven, real world, applicable advice that anyone who is serious about reinventing themselves or repackaging themselves at work can greatly benefit from.

From forming mastermind groups to searching for a mentor, Fogel lays out in detail how to give yourself the best return on your time and resources.

This is NOT your dad's stodgy business book. You know, the ones that are sometimes loaded with hyperbole, false hope, or pie-in-sky misinterpretations of what you can truly accomplish. Not by a long shot.

The author, an affable and funny fellow, infuses his how-to material with directness, humor, and easy-to-follow common sense steps for the boss or worker who wants to reboot or "repackage themselves" for a meaningful career.

Along with a brief review at the end of each chapter, Fogel smartly breaks up each chapter with detailed advice for the employee and the boss that feeds off of each other.

Why? Because Fogel knows that a combative environment between employees and bosses is not in the best interests of both parties.

He reveals to the reader the importance of how a synergy between the worker and their supervisor/boss is the quickest way for the individual and the company to grow to exciting new heights — together!

And isn't that what it's all about? Don't just read or flip through the book. Really put into motion the practical steps that are clearly outlined for you to reach career fulfillment.

I wish you continued success on your journey to the top!

Michael Masterson
Author of *Power and Persuasion: How to Command Success in Business and Your Personal Life* **www.earlytorise.com**

ABOUT THE AUTHOR

Peter "The Reinvention Guy" Fogel is a copywriter, editorialist, author, information marketer, and an "eclectic entrepreneur" (as he calls himself), who has worked and excelled in a variety of different industries.

They include surgical supply salesman, telecommunications franchise reseller, improvisational corporate speaker, international sitcom writer, stand-up comic, commercial actor, voice-over specialist, and in his earlier years, a mime. (Yes, he was young and foolish, but remarkably in the 70's "walking against the wind" paid well!)

Realizing that mimes don't have a long shelf life for reaching financial independence, Peter came to his senses and wisely entered the "secure" world of stand-up comedy.

Relentlessly honing his craft, this reformed mime became one of America's funniest comedians who you never heard of — but saw countless times on many late night comedy shows.

Luckily, having success as a comic allowed Peter to reveal to his parents, years later, that he, in fact, never did go to law school... but thanked them for the tuition money, anyway!

As an award winning humorist, he has appeared on such programs as *Caroline's Comedy Hour*, *CBS Morning Show*, *Comic Strip Live*, *Evening at the Improv*, *Rick Dees' Into the Night*, and *HBO's Comedy Central*, to name just a few.

As an in-audience warm-up in Hollywood, he has worked on such sitcoms as *Married With Children*, *Unhappily Ever After*, *Men Behaving Badly* (Rob Schneider), *Whoopi* with Whoopi Goldberg, Jason Bateman's *Chicago Sons*, and *Hope and Faith* with Kelly Ripa.

From comedy clubs and performing arts centers to cruise ships and Las Vegas theaters, Peter has had the good fortune of working with or sharing the stage with such notables as:

Rita Rudner, Jimmy "J.J." Walker, Ray Romano, Stiller and Meara, Ed Asner, Shirley Jones, Robin Williams, John Davidson, Jon Stewart, Bill Maher, Harry Anderson,

George Hamilton, The Mommies, Howie Mandel, and legendary comic icon, Robert Klein.

Earlier on in his career, Peter had the good fortune to train in improvisational comedy under the tutelage of the late Del Close, legendary artistic director of Chicago's Second City where such luminaries as Bill Murray, John Candy, Tim Kazarinski (*Police Academy*), George Wendt (*Cheers*), and Jim and John Belushi got their start.

As a comedy writer, he has punched-up scripts for such stars as Academy Award nominee, Chazz Palminteri (*A Bronx Tale, Bullets Over Broadway*), and for such Hollywood writing teams as Blake and Jackson (*Adventures of Lois & Clark, SheSpies*).

Peter was a proud member of the elite *Warner Bros. Television Writers Comedy Workshop*, and for Columbia Tri-Star's International division, he wrote on Germany's #1 sitcom (consequently their only one), *Rita's World*.

In the commercial advertising world, Peter has shamelessly hawked products on TV and radio for such sponsors as *Mazda, American Express, Zima, Miller Lite*, and *A&W Root Beer*.

Ply him with alcohol, and he'll gloat to anyone listening that in the 80's he was the *Ring Around the Collar Man for Whisk Detergent*. (Yes, he was the one with the filthy neck.)

This workaholic owes his success in the highly competitive entertainment world to having an insatiable appetite for learning how to outsell and market one's talents over the competition.

Peter accomplished this by reading books and soaking in like a sponge how business and marketing legends became uber successful, but more importantly, how adapting their laws of attraction and proven marketing strategies could help him become triumphant in his businesses!

FAST FORWARD TO AGE 40...

...and fed up with the gypsy world of show business, Peter took the plunge and entered a new stage in his life.

Taking his varied background in sales, advertising, and business, Peter pulled a 180 and reinvented himself into a copywriter/marketing consultant. His area of expertise is delivering killer promotional direct mail, and web, radio, and video copy in the self-help, financial, and self-help arenas.

Some of his multi-million dollar clients include: Rich Schefren's *Strategic Profits*, *Agora Publishing, Vital-Max Vitamins, Bio-Centric Health*, Michael Masterson's *Early to Rise, Hampshire Labs, Westhaven Labs, Dr. Al Sears, Healthier You*, and *Renaissance Health.*

When not helping his clients make boat loads of money, The Reinvention Guy is also a seminar leader and keynote speaker who gives customized presentations across the U.S and Canada.

A 2nd degree black belt in Ed Parker's Kenpo Karate, Peter uses his martial arts background and proven reinvention strategies to motivate his audiences to get out of their comfort zone and break though barriers to reach their goals.

This astute entrepreneur's highly rated presentations include actionable content along with loads of humor, of course. Peter's specialty is showing companies, associations, and entrepreneurs how to boost their profits through brand awareness, public speaking, and effective direct response and guerilla marketing techniques.

Peter is also in great demand with his hysterical motivational keynotes that show audiences how to not only survive, but thrive using humor to overcome adversity in the workplace.

He is the author of the amazon.com best seller, *If Not Now ... Then When? Stories and Strategies of People Over 40 Who Have Successfully Reinvented Themselves.*

His articles have appeared in such trade magazines as *Inside Direct Mail, DM News, and Mequoda Library.*

Peter is also a proud member of the *Writers Guild of America* and *The National Speakers Association.* He has contributed to copywriter legend, Bob Bly's books, *Persuasive Business Talks, The World's Best Kept Copywriting Secrets, Secrets to Alternative Health Copywriting Secrets.*

In addition, his comedy material has been quoted in the *Comedy Quote Dictionary* (Double Day, 1992).

My first manuscript was called, *If Not Now... Then When? Stories and Strategies of People Over 40 Who Have Successfully Reinvented Themselves.* (Yes, I am working on a longer title.)

That book focused primarily on folks over 40 (or 39.5 years of age), who for one reason or another (usually sanity, health reasons, or both), needed to leave their current gig and go into a new career that would fulfill them.

Surprisingly, a lot of these "reinventors" made their dream possible by entering the world of music, theatre, and art as entrepreneurs... the same activities they did as children!

I wrote *If Not Now... Then When?* with the aim of helping Boomers (with what was left of their 401K's) make the transition to other rewarding careers that gave them peace and satisfaction.

But then I began to wonder about the other hardworking folks out in the workforce, the folks who desire change within their chosen careers and who do NOT want to exit their present place of employment, or make a lateral move to another company.

What about the cubicle jockey who pins photos of the loved ones onto corkboards, along with the charming chicken scratch artwork their four year old did for them?

What about the worker (or manager) who was recently laid off from their job and is feverishly looking to get back into the game, but wants to make new changes to the way they are perceived at work?

What about the backbone of America — the employee — who doesn't mind daily commutes, the health benefits and $5000 deductibles, along with the "Not So Happy Hour" drinks with colleagues down at their local watering hole?

I am talking, of course, about *The Team Member — you —* who wants a regular paycheck and promotions, but you still want to reinvent yourself where you are right now at your present job.

Which is exactly why I wrote *Reboot Your Career*. And one of the most important tips I can give you, that I learned from interviewing the folks from my first book, is this:

If you want to quickly soar to new heights in your present career... if you want challenges that get you excited about your contributions at work... if you want to reach your financial goals... then to make this dream a reality, you have to think of yourself as an entrepreneur at the company you work for!

No, that's not a typo. I meant intrapreneur, not to be confused with an entrepreneur (similar, but a tad different).

Michael Masterson, self-made millionaire and publisher of *Early to Rise* states, an intrapreneur has the same smarts, motivation, goal setting, and thirst for financial independence as does an entrepreneur, but with one major difference.

Intrapreneurs do NOT feel comfortable going out on their own (as do their first cousins, entrepreneurs). Instead, they flourish by helping the companies they work for to grow exponentially by leaps and bounds!

And please note that when I mention entrepreneurship throughout this book, I am referring to you as an *intrapreneur*, the reliable, forward thinking worker (or boss) who craves to be part of something larger than themselves.

Intrapreneurs also reveal strong leadership ability and will do everything they can to help build divisions, rather than starting from scratch and starting their own businesses.

They have a strong desire to be a Star or Superstar in their company without having to make a lateral move onto a new career or greener pastures.

According to my present mental health professional, entrepreneurs are wired a little differently than most folks. (And I mean that in a good way.)

To understand this better, it's best first to define what an entrepreneur is since there is no dictionary definition of an intrapreneur. According to Wikipedia:

...an entrepreneur is someone who has possession of a new enterprise, venture or idea and assumes significant accountability for the inherent risks and the outcome.

The beauty of having an entrepreneurial zeal is that it invigorates you and gets you jazzed about taking calculated risks.

Having one gets you busy strategizing about how to bring yourself the quickest and most effective ROI on your time, money, and other resources.

Entrepreneurs, (for the most part), are optimists. They see opportunity where others see dire straits and gloom. They don't blame outside forces on their lack or otherwise of happiness, or if and when they reach financial independence doing what they love doing.

In a nutshell, entrepreneurs have a fire burning in them to make a difference in themselves and in others!

As you read *Reboot Your Career*, my hope is for you to fully understand that having an entrepreneurial mindset will assist you in reaching your goals quickly and more efficiently. During your rebooting...

- You will train and discipline yourself to recognize opportunities at your present place of employment and act upon them, so it all becomes second nature to you.

- You will learn to take responsibility for your actions and to realize that setbacks are really only temporary.

- And most importantly, despite the insurmountable odds (i.e. office politics, cutbacks, etc.), you CAN discover and create for yourself your dream job and the career that goes along with it.

WHO IS THIS BOOK FOR?
It's for the worker, middle-management, supervisor, team leader, and boss who wants more and deserves more out of their career.

I tell you this here and now. If you can keep an open mind, your sense of humor, and take specific action, reinvention can be quite exhilarating.

Just think, by following the tips, tricks, and strategies I have outlined, you, too, can shed your skin and morph into the career person you want to be! (Bigger cubicle by the window is optional.)

Alright then, let's get this party started as I reveal how rebooting your career can pay back many dividends to you and your company!

Peter "The Reinvention Guy" Fogel
Author - Speaker - Seminar Leader
www.reinventyourselfnow.com

WHAT IS YOUR CONTRIBUTION AT WORK?

"The difference between a successful person
and others is not a lack of strength,
not a lack of knowledge, but rather a lack of will..."

—Vince Lombardi

(Dead Football Coach who looked remarkably like Ernest Borgnine)

Let us begin with asking you point-blank: Are you content in your work?

I know, to some that's a loaded question. Your response might be, "Well, right now, it's 9:33 AM... check back with me at 5:00!"

Well, here's the thing, depending on how old you are, your parents or grandparents might never have even thought of asking themselves that question.

Of course, "back then" times were different for your parents, and it could have been a challenge for your grandparents.

That's because, back then when grandparents were young, they walked miles in the snow to school with a ton of rocks tied to their back, all while pulling a 52 Chevy by their teeth!

Yes, sir. In the good old days of yesteryear, when gas was forty cents a gallon, there was no real thought of enjoying your job or career. You just did it because it was... your job! That's why!

When pressed to answer the question, arguably your grandfather might reply (in that husky, no-sense, old codger's voice):

> "It's a job. You're not supposed to like it... damn it! You're supposed to work so you can pay your bills, put your damn kids through college, and then die with completely unfulfilled dreams. That's the way I did it... my father did it... and his father did it. And by golly, you're gonna do it. Now stop your bellyaching and hand me my Maalox!"

This Is NOT Your Dad's Job, Is It?!

Well, that was then, and this is now! Unfortunately, for millions of Americans these days, if you asked them if they enjoyed "the job", I bet their answer would be (if they still have a job) a resounding "No!"

According to a survey of 5,000 people conducted by marketing services company TNS, less than half of the workers were satisfied with their jobs way back in the stone age year of 2007.

Chances are, since you picked up this book, you are one of those people. The problem is what do you do about it?

Well, here are some options. Grin and bear it until one day you snap like a postal employee and the SWAT team is called in, whereupon neighbors and coworkers will invariably say,

"She was quiet and usually kept to herself. Guess it was the job!"

Or on the other hand, you could take the initiative and look for another job, but those are difficult to come by. Last year in the U.S., the unemployment rate was around 9.5% (and rising).

Yes, recession and layoffs are hot topics in the news today. By the time you look for a new gig, your job could be outsourced to a call center in India.

Here's a Dose of Hard Reality!

By the time you are reading this book, hopefully economic times will have improved. Of course, nobody has to tell you that this was your predictable, economic downturn. Not by a long shot.

Unfortunately, in today's global economy, the tables have turned. It's a buyer's market for employers. Do your research and you'll discover there are more candidates than positions. The problem is employers know this and they're structuring their pay scale accordingly.

The plain truth is even though some pundits say the job market is recovering, salary offers are many years behind.

According to ReadyMinds, a Lyndhurst N.J. provider of online career counseling and coaching, workers who were used to pulling in $100,000 a year in salary are now coming in at $85,000 or $90,000. And workers used to getting $40,000 to $50,000 are now being offered $28,000 to $38,000.

Alas, in today's job market and soft hiring market, companies are not as worker friendly as they used to be.

These days, they're focused on margins, profitability, and cutting costs any which way they can. Ask your friends and colleagues and they'll undoubtedly tell you they're doing the work of two to three people now. The situation is what it is.

Further research from Readyminds says that hiring departments are being instructed to set budgets at a lower range.

Damned If You Do... And Damned If you Don't... So Damn the Torpedoes!

To take a lower paying job offer in your field or stay unemployed... that is the question before many Americans today. Regrettably, some folks don't have a nest egg built up.

They also do NOT want to stay on unemployment, which is understandable. Folks with a good work ethic believe, and perhaps rightly so, that there's a stigma attached to being without employment. And because they feel this way, they leap onto the lower paying job.

On the flipside, there are workers who are of the opinion their current skill level translates into current wages and hold out too long for the perfect gig that pays better.

Oh, yes. It's nice to have a healthy ego about what you bring to the table. But common sense dictates you face reality regarding what your current job salary is in your area of expertise.

Walter Akana, a career strategist in Decatur, Georgia, suggests that if you've been out of work for a long time, then it might be prudent to accept the lower paying job offer— for now.

And if you do, experts say workers can ask about educational and training opportunities. Now, if you do accept a low offer, make sure you're gaining in other ways. Do your best to make sure you get valuable experience or access to a network that can advance your career.

In life and in business, you don't get what you deserve, you get what you negotiate!

You can rest easy. In later chapters I address how to negotiate properly with your employer to get the appropriate cool perks that others might not get.

For now, let's assume you have a job and have even looked for greener pastures, and during your search, you couldn't find a suitable position where the pay was comparable to your present job.

More often than not, there are firms offering promising positions — the old "I'll dangle the carrot in front of you" during the interview process. But you are required to take the dreaded pay cut.

On the other hand, you may be of the mindset that you just don't want to go through the trouble of dusting off the resume and pounding the pavement again. No, in today's corporate buying market, you don't want to become another statistic.

You don't want to spend downtime at a Starbucks with Wi-Fi (pretending it's your office) and then pounding the pavement with hurt feet while lamenting,

> "Yippee! Rejection Street here I come!"

Of course, there's always this to obsess about — what happens if you land a new job in a similar industry, and although it seems different enough, there are things about it that eerily remind you of the old job?! (SFX: Cue up spooky music!)

All of a sudden, the new job becomes like that old episode of Star Trek (Sci Fi television series) where Kirk is transported to an alternate universe on the *Starship Enterprise*. (To make matters worse, on *this* Enterprise, Spock is evil and has a goatee.) In Kirk's alternative world, everything is the same — but radically different.

Oh, NO! I Changed Jobs, But NOW I'm in Bizarro World!

So there you are at your new job, excited about the future, been told what you can expect from your superior, and this happens.

Yes, you are at a different firm, with a different staff, within the same industry, but... but... everything seems "vaguely familiar."

> "MY GOD! It's like I never left the old job... it's the same!"

You pound your head with your fists to make this an even more dramatic moment and then wail to the heavens,

> "Why did I leave?!"

What you have done, my friend, is make the dreaded LATERAL MOVE! The bane of any working stiffs existence! NOW, you're the proverbial dog chasing your own tail. You think,

> "OH NO! What did this head hunter do to me? She swore this would be a better situation for me! I am back where I started! HHHHHHHHHHHHELP!" (cue up: ECHO side affect!)

And what is the alternative, you ask? How can you really be fulfilled without making a radical move to a new company?

Well, try this on for size. Let's say, for argument's sake, that you actually like your company and believe in its vision for the future. In fact, because you're such a patient person you even tolerate your co-workers without creating voodoo dolls in their images.

So then you make the decision to stay put. BUT just like a marriage you might be in, you somehow feel that deep down something is missing.

As you might know, a marriage has its ups and down and is NOT perfect. Well, it's the same with your job! And just like a marriage, if you really want something, you're going to have to do your part to keep it exciting and sexy. An example of this would be requesting of your spouse (just for that night), to wear new lingerie and pumps... whether he wants to or not.

With the decision to bring back the romance to the job, you make strategic moves to make the environment more challenging and exciting (sans lingerie and pumps).

Alright, it's gut check time, because deep down you know what you have to do! And that's...

To efficiently reinvent yourself internally
— so you can get what you want externally!

Now, before we go any further, allow me to put your mind at ease.

This isn't one of those books that's going to show you how to fire your boss by becoming an Internet millionaire, or starting a chinchilla farm. (Been there, done that! Need a chinchilla? Then please contact me.)

No, this book has a *higher* reason for being. I wrote it as a succinct guide to show you how to reinvent your current career — in your current place of employment.

That's right (feel free to exhale), you don't have to go to another company or strike out on your own to have a happy, successful career.

Isn't that great? *Reboot* is your one-stop shop to getting what you want right now! Yes, you CAN create a work environment that you LOVE where coworkers stop you and declare,

> "Great pitch this morning, Laura... everyone loved it!"

> "WOW! Right on the money, Laura. I wish I came up with that idea."

> "Now, THAT'S thinking out of the box! Congratulations, Laura!"

You're so jazzed at the recognition, it doesn't even bother you that your name isn't Laura. *But that's not the point!* The point is **your** colleagues acknowledged you. And that's what is so cool!

The plain truth is that I wrote *Reboot Your Career* for the rank and file folks like yourself who keep the engine of the machine — their company — going!

But I also wrote it for the bosses and management. Where appropriate, I've got special sections just for "the suits" as you're affectionately called behind your backs.

Here you, too, can evaluate what you're doing (and in some cases, what you're not doing) to motivate and get the people to stay who can make your job easier. And isn't that what everyone wants at their company?

Do You Have a Contribution Statement?

Let's examine what I mentioned earlier in my introduction. The concept of being in business for yourself (an intrapreneur) within the company you work for.

As an entrepreneur, I discovered if I wanted to truly succeed and reap the benefits of my efforts, I needed to effectively promote my business as well as my clients. To do that I had to create a powerful USP, which is short for **Unique Selling Proposition.**

In a nutshell, a USP highlights within the eyes of your prospect, you're different and more desirable than your competition.

One sure-fire way to come up with a USP for your most important product (you) is to write down the benefits that make you so darn special!

Owning your USP and getting it out into the marketplace (your company) will allow you to shine in the eyes of your bosses. Better yet, it could invariably help you reach your career goals a lot sooner than you ever thought possible!

Now, before you put energy into creating your USP, you should first focus on building a strong foundation that can support it.

To do that, you absolutely must be clear on what your career goals are. (I know, easier said than done, right?) But what happens if you have a "strong inkling" of those goals, but nothing really leaps out at you?

Well, to overcome Career Path Block (CPB), you have to dig deep within yourself and really see what inspires you to make an impression on yourself and your company. The way to do that is to create a **Contribution Statement**.

According to Stephen Covey, your Contribution Statement sums up the best of what you have to offer to the challenges that excite you. It becomes the rudder of your career.

The exciting part of creating and working off a **Contribution Statement** is that it will (a) help push you in the right direction to excel in your career, and (b) help skyrocket your brand within your industry. (Later on we'll also talk about branding and its importance.)

The one thing you don't want to put all your focus on in regards to career goals is (drum roll, please), "The Promotion"!

Yes, I'm quite aware that a promotion means more prestige — a new business card, more money, and of course, the opportunity to now park your car closer and NOT in the remote company parking located miles away.

But you're getting ahead of yourself. Here's what I mean.

Let's say you have a very high opinion of yourself and what you do at the job. In fact, you've been "on the job" for a whopping six months and NOW you're getting antsy. In fact, you think because you've put your time in, by golly, it's NOW time to announce to the world:

> "Hey, what does a person have to do around here to get a promotion for crying out loud? (beat) Hello, is anybody there? Does anyone hear me? (longer pause; starts to whimper) Does anyone ... really ... hear me?!"

Yes, this book is about helping you reach career nirvana, but having an elitist attitude so early on while working at your new job is probably not going to get you what you want.

Instead of letting the world know you want Bill's corner office because he got canned and justifying your squatter's rights by saying, "Well, it's empty and no one else is using it", perhaps you should put your energies into thinking:

How can I **(INSERT NAME)** make a profound contribution to my company **(INSERT NAME)** which could be my lasting legacy?

Notice how much more powerful that is?

That's because owning a potent Contribution Statement will put your career goals in motion.

Taking this particular path will also put you on the radar of *The Almighty Promotion Gods!* (SFX: CRACK of THUNDER) And you never want to upset *The Almighty Promotion Gods*, do you? (SFX: More THUNDER and now LIGHTNING!)

Let's now return to you and your Contribution Statement. Do you have one lurking around in your head? Here's mine, and perhaps it will get your creative juices flying.

> "My goal is to treat my client's product or service as if it's my own. Doing so will allow me to create persuasive killer copy that delivers a strong ROI for that client!"

For my corporate speaking clients:

> "To deliver actionable content to my audience that not only motivates them but allows them to reach their goals more swiftly and effectively!"

Let's examine some others that might kick-start your imagination from the book, *Great Work, Great Career* by Stephen R. Covey and Jennifer Colosimo:

> "If someone needs a helicopter to fly higher or faster than it does today, it's up to me to find the materials that can take the heat and stress that kind of performance would put on a helicopter engine."
> -Katherine Bicer, Materials Engineer

> "Give women the message that smarts is beautiful... to prevent today's looks-obsessed women from developing eating disorders... to encourage younger women that it's about who you are as a person, not just about how you look."
> -Dr. Vidushi Babber, Physician and Educator

"Improve working conditions for employees so they suffer from less pain and get fewer injuries while on the job. I would do this by creating a positive environment that encourages safety and teamwork."
-**Brian Ness, Safety Engineer**

Zig Ziglar, the great motivational speaker, once said if you want to reach your goals, discover how to help others reach theirs first. For your whole career, and even for specific projects, you should create a succinct **Contribution Statement.**

As a copywriter, whenever I begin a project for a client I create a copy platform first. It's an extensive outline that breaks down the components of the project.

It helps show the client that we are on the same page (literally) of how I am going to approach writing his sales promotion. Doing this prevents us from having any ambiguity about the sales letter's USP, pricing, guarantee, offer, etc.

The final stage is to have my client sign off on it. Creating a Contribution Statement for yourself is similar. Of course, you don't have to have your supervisor sign off on it, but you should seriously lean towards using one for your own needs.

In fact, you'll be amazed at how it will give you a laser like focus and propel you forward to helping you achieve career satisfaction, or finishing off your own individual projects.

Don't Let This Happen to You!

Over the years, I'm proud to say I've talked to many people in different careers about their career choice(s). You see, I love to know what makes people tick, or why they gravitate towards a specific field or niche.

Sometimes, choosing a career may seem right for you at a certain stage of your working life. At other times, you'll discover you will want a change or a tweaking of your choice.

For instance, I have a buddy named Dan who made excellent money working as a money manager for a big, corporate, behemoth bank that got bailed out by Uncle Sam during the housing crisis. (Back then, who didn't?)

Anyway, Dan has been grinding away at this profession for close to 20 years. And guess what? Now he wants to try to become a professional comedian. He loves it. It drives him, but I warned him,

"Dan, the party is over for making the big money in stand-up... the boom has gone bust!"

He replied, "Yeah, I know... but I gotta try. I love making people laugh!"

My friend has got the comedy bug, big time. (I know the feeling.) Then I said,

"What about your great career, the money, the office, the overpriced European sports car the company pays for?"

Shaking his head, Dan replied,

"Pete, it's stressful. Every day I live and die by the stock market... every day I have to answer to my clients... every day..."

And his voice would trail off. Sadly, I knew exactly what he meant.

He is now a full-time comedian working part-time as a money manager with a few close clients.

As you know, in business everything is timing, which is why this is the perfect time to introduce our next chapter. It deals with a subject that I'm sure is near and dear to your heart and probably one of the reasons you bought this book!

"Not only do we have a great retirement program, our employees age more quickly."

CHAPTER 1:

Your Happiness is Your Job

"I am not the boss of my house. I don't know when I lost it.
I don't know if I ever had it.
But I have seen the boss's job and I do not want it."

—Bill Cosby

Tell me if this is happening to you. You've been working in your job for a few years now. Like any relationship, in the beginning it was great. Your work was challenging and exciting.

You liked the people you worked with. Life was good. You felt fulfilled! (A la a preacher.)

"Can you give me a hallelujah?!"

Then, as I mentioned earlier, you started feeling like something was missing. Your job became mind-numbingly boring, and your coworkers constantly got on your nerves.

You started thinking to yourself,

"I don't want to be a widget remover (or insert the name of your job description) for the rest of my life."

Perhaps you even started to wonder if you made the right decision by coming to this company.

You know what? That's okay. You see, our situations change, and the reasons we wanted something might not be as strong in hindsight as they were in the beginning.

Thankfully, there's something you can do about it.

Now, what I'm about to say just may get under your skin a little bit. I'm sorry, but it's necessary if we are to move forward.

It may sound crazy, but it's true: **If our work helps define us— then happiness is your job.** What an epiphany, huh? We can now release the balloons and fireworks!

❖ 36 ❖

Now you might be kickin' and screamin', but happiness is your number one priority. It is NOT your boss's or your coworkers; it's yours. And if you are going to make a real and sustainable change, you must realize that fact.

Now, don't beat yourself up for not realizing this sooner. Here's the thing...

We're all taught from an early age that everything, absolutely everything we want or even need in life is ours for the taking, just because of the simple fact that we exist.

Our parents subconsciously spread this vicious lie and our schools reinforce it. From day one, we're made to believe that we can have, do, or be whatever we want without having to work for it, or make ourselves worthy of receiving it.

Then, when we get out into the real world, we find out just how vicious this lie is. It's not your fault you were made to think this way. (Here, take a tissue and dab your eyes and let out a good blow.)

Feeling better? Good. Now, just because you were taught this from birth doesn't mean you have to keep living your life as if it's the truth.

Repeat after me, por favor:

> "Everything I have in my life is my fault. Not my boss's, not the government's. Not the economy. I am 100% responsible for me and my actions."

Oh, God, I know this is hard to admit. But aren't we just a little programmed to blame our misfortune on everybody else? (And doesn't it feel better when we do?)

I mean, it is so much easier to rant about someone else than beat yourself up. Although, at times, I do both.

Oh, sure there are some things that are out of our control, but for the most part, it really is up to you, isn't it? Let me make this clear.

I'm not telling you this to make you feel bad about yourself, but to show you how much power you have over your situation.

YES! I am giving YOU the authority to change your situation! And I must be serious, because I just italicized that last sentence.

Look at it this way. If you give yourself permission to be responsible for everything that has happened to you in your life, especially all the bad stuff, then you can change it!

You can turn your situation around, without relying on some outside force like the government, luck, fate, or karma to do it for you.

Doesn't that feel great? Doesn't that make you feel more in control? Start thinking about everything that you can do to turn your life around before you start blaming yourself for all your past mistakes. Again, it is okay! We've all been there. (Oh, have I been there!)

Because here's another thing... Not to go all Zen on you, *but all we have is now*. This moment right here. The past is gone. The future isn't here... yet. Therefore, you might as well focus on now and start from there... I mean, here! (You get the idea.)

You Are Here

You know those maps at the mall that show you where everything is? Every one of them has a big dot that says "You Are Here" so that people know where they are in relation to everything the mall offers. For argument's sake, let's say you are that dot.

"You are Here" and nothing you can do will change your location right this second. But, where you go from here is entirely, completely up to you.

So, what does all this have to do with being happy, you ask? In a word, everything.

See, while we were being taught that we would one day have everything we've ever wanted handed to us on a silver plate, we were also being programmed to believe that happiness and other emotions come from things outside ourselves.

In other words, we are *made* happy or sad, angry or frustrated, by a *thing* that has been given to us. As if the object itself came with those emotions attached to it. And it is our job to then *feel* whatever that thing is doing to us.

I am sure you know what I am talking about. Something happens — you didn't get the promotion, or a project at work went to someone else, even though you put months of research into it.

You curse, you vent, wondering if there's a conspiracy against you ever succeeding. (One of my favorite pastimes, by the way.)

You curse the heavens, get drunk, and possibly wake up in strange places like Tijuana (again!).

The culprit at work here — your mind and the baggage that comes with it — is assigning value and meaning to this particular thing or harrowing event.

And if I was Dr. Phil right now, besides thanking my lucky stars that I kissed Oprah's butt enough to get his show, I'd look right into the camera and say (with a Texan drawl),

> "The truth is, you and I can choose to feel any way we want about whatever happens to us. (SFX: Studio Audience Applauds) And now a word from our sponsor, Tic-Tacs. (SFX: More Studio Audience Applause)"

You deal with challenges and frustrations. Well, no one has had more success or dealt with more challenges than Thomas Edison had inventing the light bulb. Perhaps you know the story.

Edison toiled for years and went through thousands of tries before he created the first prototype of the light bulb. When someone asked him if he had failed, Thomas quipped,

> "I didn't fail. I just learned thousands of ways how not to make a light bulb."

Then I believe Edison tried to sell the guy a used Victrola he had listed on e-Bay that no one bid on.

Once again, your feelings are your own. You worked for them, you put in your time, and if you want to blow off steam and good fortune, do it and get it over with, and know once again, that you can quickly react to events differently.

I would hope you choose how you want to interpret events. If something is bothering you, figure out how you can make it better instead of complaining about it and giving up.

Picking certain times to vent or blow off steam can be a good thing and lower your blood pressure. And no one vents and yells to the heavens more than your dear author here.

Remember: Obsessing about something (no matter how great it feels) will NOT get you closer to achieving your goal.

So, how do you begin the process of reaching your goals then? You simply begin by making a list. That's right, a list... but with this criterion: This time you should make it a group effort and enlist your friends and significant (or insignificant) other to help you.

In the cliff Note version, you basically want to jot down:

- What you love about your job and what bugs you.
- Something from your latest performance review that you need to improve on and the steps needed to improve it.
- A list of all the options that are at your disposal.
- What is possible and what isn't, given your organization's leadership, culture, and rules.
- Anybody who may be able to help you get where you want to be.
- Any skills you are lacking and the steps you'll take to learn them.

Good, go do it. (I'll wait.) No cheating, really do it. If you don't, we'll all know you didn't. (Looks at watch.) Okay class, time's up... pencils down!

Now here's the good part. Look over what you just wrote and know that NOW you're armed with some real knowledge. Now you can help yourself set goals and motivate yourself to do what you need to do.

Take Care of Business, Your Own!

Here's what I mean. If you've figured out your company's rules and culture won't support the change you want to make, then you'll know ahead of time. Then you can plan something different.

Remember, if you don't know where you're going, any road will take you there!

And now...

FOR BOSSES
You didn't think I was going to leave you out, did you? You, my friend, are quite important to your subordinates. For any bosses reading this, this section is for you.

While it's true every individual on your team are adults and responsible for how they got their present position, you are still their supervisor, manager, or Big Kahuna.

That said, and whether you want to admit to it or not, you have somewhat of a stake in their continued happiness.

So, ask yourself right now, are you working to make sure your employees feel fulfilled, rewarded, and getting what they want out of their work? If not, why not?

WHAT IT'S COSTING YOU

By now you're probably saying in a gruff, managerial, "old school" voice (similar to your angry grandparent's voice that I did earlier),

> "But I don't have time for all this 'fluff.' I've got a division to run. I have my own challenges. I DO NOT have time to give hugs! When I was coming up there were no hugs given out. Listen here, if my employees want something, I trust them to come right out and tell me."

But are they? If not, it doesn't necessarily mean that they're all firing-on-all-cylinders happy. Whether or not you give it your attention, there could be some real problems that you won't even know about until it's too late.

All it costs you is a little of your "sweat equity" on your time. (Hugs optional.) Don't have it, you say? Well, let's look at what not doing anything is costing you and your company in terms of employee turnover with some number crunching, shall we?

As you're aware, numbers don't lie. (Unless it's the government's numbers.) According to a U.S. Department of Labor study, it costs one-third of an $8 an hour employee's annual salary to replace them.

This includes direct costs such as advertising, sign on bonuses, recruiter fees, and overtime for all the workers it takes to do that person's job until you can find someone else.

Let's now throw in indirect costs like recruitment, selection, training, and decreased productivity while your current employees pick up the slack.

Remarkable, for someone making only 8 bucks an hour!

According to a study conducted by the *Bureau of National Affairs* (www.bna.com), the turnover costs for a $40,000 per year employee is 70% of his or her annual salary, or $28,000.

Oh, and let's not forget absenteeism. The BNA found that absenteeism ranges from 2% to 6%, depending on the industry, and can cost an average of $660 per employee for each missed day of work. Ouch!

It's NOT Just About the Money ... Or is It?

When managers are polled about how they attract and keep good employees, most of them say 'money' without fail. Ah, the greenbacks... the dead presidents... the moolah.

These managers put all the responsibility for keeping their star players in the hands of senior management and blame pay scales or the policies of the organization when staff start moving to other departments or jumping ship.

Yes, money talks, but it's never entirely about money. Ready for this, my dear upper management friend? Study after study has found that all employees want the same basic things:

▌ Meaningful, challenging work
▌ A chance to learn and grow
▌ Fair compensation
▌ A good work environment
▌ Respect from colleagues, bosses, and supervisors

Think about it. Doesn't everyone want those things? Don't you? And yet, it's surprising how many employees are out there who aren't getting all of these things from their job.

If it's to Be — It's Up to ME!

So, what can you do to turn the tide of rampant turnover and employees who call in sick more often than Ferris Bueller? (*Ferris Bueller's Day Off* is a 1986 American teen coming-of-age comedy film.)

● **Commit Yourself to Employee Satisfaction and Retention**

Read the tips I am giving you in this book, then pick at least one strategy to implement this month.

● **Get the Whole Team Involved**

If you have managers and supervisors under you, get them on board. And here's a splendid idea and shameless plug — give them all a copy of this book!

If they want, they can come up with ways they can be held accountable for the teams and divisions they manage. Hold monthly meetings to discuss what strategies they are implementing and scrutinize the results.

● **Talk to Your People on the Front Lines**

Communicate with your employees on a routine basis. And yes, you should, dare I say, get to know them as people, not just as employees.

<u>Reinvention Guy's Take-Away Tip</u>: Have a care-free, cocktail partyesque conversation with your team member/worker. Push yourself if you have to. Ask them about their families, their hobbies, and what their career goals are. (And not through e-mail either, please!) You may be pleasantly surprised as to what you hear.

And above all else, don't be afraid of what you find out. Oh, and guess what? As their leader, you just may discover plenty of ways you can help these folks (who make YOUR job, hopefully, easier and more fulfilling), reach their attainable goals.

And if not, at least you'll get to know them better and make them feel like a valuable part of the company.

Okay, Class... Let's Review!

To make yourself happy at work:

■ Take 100% responsibility for everything in your life, good and bad.
■ List the things you don't like about your job. This could be your performance, or what is and isn't possible for you given your company's culture and rules.
■ Then list the names of anyone who has your back and can help you with the skills you need to improve yourself or improve upon, or a brand new needed skill that will add to your Contribution Statement.

FOR THE BOSSES
■ Realize it isn't just about the money. Just like our spouses, employees have other important needs and desires.
■ Commit yourself to employee satisfaction and retention.
■ Get the whole team involved to assist in staff retention.
■ Talk to your people and find out what makes them tick. (Hugs optional.)

Is everything starting to make sense to you about how every worker and manager should synergistically work together? Well, we're just getting started.

Our next chapter examines the most important person in your life and how they are going to help you reboot your career. Do you know who that is?

"No need to call me Mr. Bigge, T. M. We're all on a first and second initial basis around here."

CHAPTER 2:
Assess Yourself

"The unexamined life is not worth living."

— **Socrates (dead philosopher)**

Now that we've gotten all that uncomfortable, yet liberating, stuff out of the way, our next step is to figure out exactly what you actually want.

Let's get back to the most important subject there is — YOU! And to do that we need to assess you and your present career.

Life and business continually throw us curves. Just like any new relationship, we sometimes go into a job thinking it's exactly what we "thought" we wanted.

Fast forward a few years into it, and we start to feel like something is wrong. Something is missing.

You might ask yourself,

"Do I really want to be a cube monkey for the rest of my life?"

Then it happens. The thoughts start twirling in our head. This leads to us doing crazy things to "replace" whatever it is we think we've "lost."

Our spouses think we're having a midlife crisis. Our bosses think we're slacking off. We think we're going a little nuts as we pop another Xanax to calm our frayed nerves.

Guess what? I'm here to tell you it isn't as bad as all that. Look, if you're starting to feel like your career is going to hell in a hand basket, here are a few things you can do.

Consult Your Inner Child!

First off, you need to digress for a moment. No really, I mean it. Digress! Now, turn back the clock. What did you want to be when you grew up? Maybe you wanted to be a doctor, a lawyer, a ballerina, cowboy, or a werewolf hunter/vampire slayer.

Whatever it was, however silly it may seem now, are you honestly any closer to that life now?

Has your vision met your reality? Many times, what we want to be just doesn't seem "practical" or to jive with our parent's vision for us.

Our parents admonish us with the usual,

> "Listen, STOP with this dream of fulfillment… dreaming of fulfillment does NOT pay the bills! You need to get a steady job that offers decent money and benefits instead!"

Take it from me, dear reader, nothing brings more joy to a young man's parent's hearts than paying for their son's four year college education, only to have him performing, years later, as a comedian at Uncle Ho's Comedy Hut in Akron, Ohio.

Of course, THAT was my initial journey. But I hope you'll agree, for the most part a lot of us listen to our parents, because the "inner petulant child" inside us wants to please them, only to discover when we did, it didn't complete them.

I can't tell you how many friends of mine went to law school as a *fallback career* only to end up never practicing law.

So, here's the drill: instead of becoming a writer, we became an insurance adjuster. Instead of a nurse, we became a massage therapist.

Now, before you get defensive and start sending me more hate e-mail than my own immediate family, know there's absolutely nothing wrong with any of those career choices.

Ah! But there was nothing necessarily wrong with your dream, either, young Skywalker — now was there?! Except, of course, "the werewolf hunter thing" (proving once again a poor career choice due to the small market of available werewolves).

Anyway, psychologists call what I have just described "expectancy violation." This twelve-dollar phrase happens when people decide to do something important in their lives — then fail to follow through with it.

If that is you, please don't be hard on yourself. Certain circumstances might have prevented you from reaching a particular dream — family, unexpected illness, etc.

For a long time, I really wanted to leave show business, but like Al Pacino said in *The Godfather*,

"Every time I try to get out... they just pull me back in!"

Let's examine some particular "expectancy violations."Perhaps, you wanted to write the great American novel and took up a career in teaching instead. To put it mildly, it's as if you have defaulted on a contract with your subconscious mind, which can cause depression, restlessness, and feelings of inferiority.

Does this sound like anything you've gone through lately? (DING! DING! We have a winner!) If so, then I have the cure.

Start a Career Journal (Oh, NO! Homework!)

No really, this will be fun! A career journal will allow you to review those old contracts with yourself. They help you realize that those "contracts" are just expectations you set for yourself when you were younger and enable you to evaluate them to see if they still hold up these days.

Begin by thinking about your earliest memories and feelings surrounding the word "work". Are they happy? Sad? Confused? What images does it conjure up?

We first learn about the world of work from our parents. Did they come home from work happy? Energetic? Tired? Angry? Did your folks complain about their boss or coworkers? Or were they always excited about whatever project they were working on?

For the longest time, my father did nothing but bitch and moan about "his job"... the problems he was having with "the Business" ... blaming everything on the doctors. (The business was a surgical supply store that dealt with foot traffic customers, hospitals, and physicians.)

Now for the surprising part: *he owned the company*. The man just loved to complain about everything, and yet, did nothing to change his reality!

Sadly, as brilliant a man as he was (he had something like four degrees including a doctorate and law degree), he did NOT realize that he had all the control to change the way he reacted to a business HE owned!

My father, unfortunately, had mental health problems and was a bully to his staff who he continually hired and fired over the years.**

** My siblings and I worked in the family business over the years. We soon came to the realization that vacationing in hell while getting a colonoscopy without anesthesia was more desirable.**

So, as you can well imagine, and it should be no surprise to you, that yes —

Your first assumptions about work were formed by watching your parents.

At eleven years of age, I was savvy enough to know that entering my father's business would shorten my life span. But what about you? What were your expectations as a child?

And if you're wondering what you should write in your journal in regards to your career reinvention, how about this?

Just write about what the word 'work' meant to you as you were first learning about its meaning.

- Think about any milestones you've had regarding your thoughts about work.
- Think about your first job, then the expectations about your future working life that you had while in high school, then your first job after college.

Alright, then. Now click your ruby slippers together and then whisk yourself ahead to the present day. So, what have you got? How have your expectations changed between then and now?

What were you promised that did or did not happen? What were you expected to be once you graduated from college? (Your expectations and other's expectations for you.)

Take Inventory... Where is Your Career Right Now?

Once you've gathered your old thoughts about work, you should evaluate where you are now. In your career journal, write down exactly what you like, what you don't like, and what needs fixing.

Think about:

- The state of your industry. Is it booming, or experiencing layoffs? (Yes, I know this is a loaded question.)
- Your job duties. Are they what you planned? Do they fulfill your personal contracts? Do they offer variety and fulfillment? Why, or why not?
- Your salary. Is it in line with your original expectations?
- Your benefits, insurance, and other "perks". We often forget about these when evaluating our current level of success, but they are extremely important.
- Your work relationships.
- Your boss. (Nice person, or a complete jerk? Or both?)

Be Honest — Where is Your Industry Heading?

As important as knowing your feelings about work and your current job are, they're only one small piece of the overall career pie we are baking. Another key ingredient is the state of your industry.

Look at the trends within this market place and honestly assess it.

- Is your industry on the way up — or on the way down? (And does it need to reposition or reinvent itself?)
- Is it growing, or experiencing massive layoffs?
- Are your friends and colleagues in the industry getting promotions, or canned while their old jobs get sent to India?
- Are they "bitching and moaning" about their situation?

What is the secret to getting the answers you so urgently need?

Simple, watch the news and read trade magazines and newspapers for stories about your industry, no matter how negative it is. Like an eagle scout, be on the lookout for downsizing and the like, and how the stock market is doing.

Talk to your friends, family, and work colleagues to see what they've heard. Keep your ear to the tracks, so you can hear the train coming and it doesn't run you over!

The beauty of all this bird dogging is these resources can help you get a handle on where your company and industry are now, and where they're headed in the future.

That Is Happening Now... BUT What About Tomorrow?

Now that you've reassessed where your industry is right now, it's time to start thinking about where it might be tomorrow. (Gulp!) As they say, "It's time to really look at the handwriting on the wall!"

It takes vision, the ability to look at something seemingly unimportant, to view its potential.

Walt Disney looked at thousands of acres of Florida swampland and saw a theme park. People refused to back him, saying things like, "No one will come to a swamp," and "Orlando, a tourist destination?" And "Why on earth are you going to freeze your head after you're dead?" (Urban myth has it that Walt cryogenically had his body frozen after his death.)

Today, millions of people a year visit Disney's five theme parks as their attraction-filled tourist destination. Through good times and bad, they stand on-line for hours on end with screaming kids just to experience "Walt's dream" of over-priced parking and food!

Bill Gates, Paul Allen, and Steve Jobs predicted that one day computers would be in every home and set out to make that happen.

<u>**Reinvention Guy's Take-Away Tip:**</u> Okay, you can relax. You don't have to be Walt or Bill. However, to experience growth within your field you should look around at things going on in and around your industry to see how it will be impacted.

Owning this inside knowledge of your career can help you figure out what to change. And just as importantly, reveal a few aspects of your current position that aren't so dreadful after all.

Maybe you've got a great 401(k) plan, or full use of the local country club. Just make sure that as you're "rebooting", you don't let go of some of those niceties you've come to rely on in your current job.

Evaluating where you are right now will also help you determine if there is anything you don't want more of, like working on weekends and holidays, or less-than-desirable job duties. Figure out what you don't want, and you'll be that much closer to figuring out what you do want.

IN REVIEW
To assess your career:

- Review your mental contracts.
- Start a career journal that can keep you on track for your short-term and long-term goals.
- Review where your career and industry are now and where it will be in the future.

Let me ask you something. If you were in your boss's proverbial shoes, knowing what you know about yourself, *would you honestly hire you based on your personal "brand"?*

"What?" you think, "Now I am a brand like Coke?" Well, the next chapter answers that question. Go on, turn the page to discover how YOUR brand is going to help you leap over the competition into your boss's consciousness!

"I'm sorry, Mr. McWit isn't here.
He's a one minute manager and
is only here from 9:00 to 9:01."

CHAPTER 3:

Want Something? Just Ask!

"He who asks is a fool for five minutes, but he who does not ask remains a fool forever."

— Ancient Chinese Proverb (Is there any other kind?)

I know, it can't be that simple, but it is. If you want something, just ask for it. Oh, and that goes for anything in work and in life, be it more job responsibilities, or a raise. Your boss is not a mind reader. How will he or she know what you want if you don't ask?

Your boss (who is at this very moment putting out lots of fires), has LOTS of things on his mind (mainly himself) and can't possibly read yours.

Sure, when the possibility for asking comes up, you might freeze and ask yourself, (gulp) "What if they say no?"

Well, I'm not going to lie to you. In this particular economic climate, there's a distinct possibility of that happening. But here's the good news, if you can find any. The outcome will depend upon a couple of factors: (a) how good an employee you are, and (b) how you ask.

Honestly— How Good An Employee Are You?

It's time to look in the mirror and NOT say (in a maniacal British accent),

"Mirror, mirror, on the wall, who's the fairest employee of them all?"

But instead, look deep within yourself and honestly assess You Inc. What kind of a worker are you? Take this simple quiz:

- Are you always at work early, or five minutes late?
- Do you leave ten minutes early? Or stay an hour late?
- Do you complain?
- Are you polite and respectful to supervisors, coworkers, and customers?
- Are you well-dressed, well groomed, and orderly?

- Do you spend your free timing boning up on your skills, or photocopying your butt? (And no, that wasn't me!)
- Is your workspace clean and free of clutter, or does your office or cubicle always look like a tornado touched down in it?

Okay, class... pencils down! What did you come up with? As I am sure you can tell, the list goes on and on. But there is one ultimate question you should always ask yourself before going to the boss to ask for more responsibility, a raise, or anything else. Ready?

Knowing what your boss now knows about you, would they hire you today?

GULP! Now, before you barge into your boss's office and demand a raise (or whatever perk you're after), honestly ask that question of yourself.

Pause for just a moment and put yourself in your boss's shoes. Walk a mile in his (or her) wingtips and see yourself through their eyes for a change.

If you don't like what you see, then guess what, my friend? It's time to make some home improvements before asking for that better position with the extra dinero that comes with it.

Why not just go to your boss and ask him or her all this? DON'T! (Tires come to a screeching halt.)

First of all, you may not like some of the answers. And second, you want to improve as many of these shortcomings as you can before going to the boss and asking for what you want. In a nutshell, you want to get your own house in order first.

Remember... to get a yes, you want to take the path of least resistance for your superior to say yes!

What is YOUR Brand?

In sales and marketing we have a term called **branding**. This is the essence of what a product or service is, or delivers to its targeted audience.

This is an important concept to understand, but more importantly to execute at work if you want to reinvent yourself in your career. People's perception of it is THEIR reality.

It brings the most important asset to the proverbial table: you!

Good examples of branding are companies like Coca-Cola, Starbucks, or UPS. What images do they conjure up? (I'll wait.) Think of the Gecko in the Geico commercials. Got it? That in a nutshell is Madison Avenue, or Institutional branding at work.

Of course, the typical corporate American worker might think they are above branding, and that all they have to do is sit in their cube like "little cube gnomes" and do their little tasks and go home. That might be them. But it's NOT you, right? They take the fatalist attitude of…

> "I'll just close my eyes and make believe I am invisible here… so as NOT to make a fuss!"

And yes, there are those unfortunate workers who simply while away the hours until quitting time and or retirement. These folks are not what you would call progressive.

They are little fish in their bowls, happy to get the morsels of food that management drops into their world from time to time… always looking at the clock… wondering how many sick days they have… or wondering how to build up more sick days so they can add it to their vacation time… scamming… scheming … working the system to suit their selfish needs.

Regrettably, they are not progressive thinking people. They don't expect greatness from themselves.

And you know what? They're not fooling anybody. That includes their colleagues, managers, or department heads. Which is why people at the company do not give them a second look, nor help them reach their true potential.

Alas, that is NOT you, is it? Well, I am betting it's not. You, who are reading this book, want to improve your working life and contribute to your present company, but you want to do it in the most efficient and cost effective way you can. This is why branding is crucial.

Branding stamps your essence into the consciousness of people around you. Your boss or your fellow workers, for better or worse, have a specific perception of what you are and what your value is.

So says, "The Reinvention Guy" which is my brand. Speakers, authors, and actors have brands or value. I have a speaker colleague who promotes holistic healing and is a life coach. He also happens to run a bartering business.

Whenever you hear his name come up in conversation, people will automatically say,

"Oh, yeah, I heard of Louis, he's that barter guy." He can't escape it, even though that is only one leg of his business.

Let's pause as I put on my black beret and turtleneck and wax philosophical for a moment... Through five decades of living (and one I can't remember, perhaps it was the disco era), I've come to realize all really big problems in life are marketing problems.

Repeat after me: all big problems in life are marketing problems.

Want the girl (or guy) to go out with you? **Marketing**. Want the girl (or guy) to marry you? **Marketing**. Want the great job? You guessed it. (Long pause.) **Marketing**.

In everything we do we are somehow marketing ourselves, our ideas, or our point of view to someone else. I even had to market this book to convince you to read it! HA!

I know you were taught as a child to NOT brag about yourself or spout off about your accomplishments. Well, guess what? NOT doing that is holding you back!

Recent experiments conducted by Haifa University researcher, Nurit Tal-Or showed the positive impact of bragging about those close to you, i.e. a family member or a colleague, versus bragging about yourself.

The results showed that people who brag about themselves are considered more competent than those who brag about others.

Here's the way you should look at it. If you've got the goods and can back it up, "effective bragging" of how you reached success can boost your career brand.

And your career brand is important when you are trying to move up in your career. Sadly, no one teaches you these techniques in business school. So (cue music), I will take this burden upon myself and hopefully put you on the right path to "effective branding".

<u>One sure-fire way to brand yourself is to make yourself MORE valuable in the eyes of your coworkers and your bosses!</u>

In Stephen Covey's and Jennifer Colosimo's book, *Great Work, Great Career* (FranklinCovey), they outline four steps that will help you do just that.

STEP 1 YOU'VE GOT TO "SELL" YOURSELF WHEN THE TIME IS RIGHT.
If you are in the elevator with your boss, now would be the perfect time to give your "elevator speech" before you reach your floor. Scary? Yes! Time to get out of your comfort zone? Absolutely.

Again, what have you produced for the company? Take inventory of what your accomplishments are. Again, **what VALUE do you bring to your company?** Be proud of your accomplishments and let The Head Suit (AKA the manager you talk to) know about it. Don't feel comfortable doing that? It's not "your thing"? Practice your elevator speech — and do it anyway!

STEP 2 FIND A SOLUTION TO THE PROBLEM. IT'S REALLY A NO-BRAINER, ISN'T IT?

Business in the 21st century is fast moving. You have to be quick on your feet to come up with "the answers" to many problems that are hitting your department, or your company in general. As I always say, with chaos comes opportunity... for you to shine, to be the one with the right answer to correct a problem, regardless how big or small!

STEP 3 BUILD A VILLAGE.

In the old days (pre-Internet), a lot of your success was determined by the dreaded office politics. And yes, it shall always be there. But you can be a Zen master and not have to play the game head-on. Instead of positioning yourself over someone, do your best to help out a colleague who is stretched to the limit. Extend yourself. These days, it truly is the little things that shine.

STEP 4 EXPAND YOUR ROLE.

Again, do you have a job? Or do you have a career? Having a job reminds me of the character George Castanza from the hit sitcom, Seinfeld.

If you watched the show then you most likely feel, as I do, that George did the minimal amount of work to get the job done.

In fact, it seems he never wanted to stand out. His fear if he did was HIS boss would catch on to what he was all about and he'd get fired. Which is why the episode of George sleeping underneath his desk was so hilarious. In his mind, hiding there allowed him to be invisible!

George lived by the adage minimal work meant minimal risk. To me, THAT'S what you do with a "job", right?

In a hilarious way, George's position with the Yankees defined him. And yet, he never really went out of his comfort zone, unless he could benefit from it. So ask yourself right now, do you wait to be told what to do?

Or do you take the initiative — stretch out of your boundaries and take the necessary actions to get out of your comfort zone? My advice is carpe diem: Seize the day — seize your opportunities, or create them yourself!

Your Personal Branding Questions

Let's return to branding. When a filmmaker directs a film or an author writes a book, their goal is to use this vehicle to brand itself into your consciousness.

A good example is the movie *Die Hard*, a film that launched a brand (or a franchise). Bruce Willis's character, a "violence magnet", is once again caught in a do or die situation where he has no choice but to save the world from evil.

But rest easy, *you* don't have to swing from a skyscraper holding a child in one arm, grasping an assault rifle in the other, bleeding and shooting at Islamic terrorists (who for some strange reason have German accents).

Instead, as you reboot your career, your goal should be working on shedding your old skin and reinventing your brand within the company.

This is true during good economic times and especially important during challenging economic times where people might be laid off at the company.

Want to make the cut and be "The Last Employee Standing?" Then take care of business and seize the opportunity.

Be a Fish out of Water

According to Robin Fisher Roffer, CEO of Big Fish Marketing in Los Angeles and author of the book *Fearless Fish Out of Water*, movers and shakers never hide who they are... they live their lives with conviction.

"If you hunker down in your cubicle and play it safe, you'll probably get a pink slip." Robin suggests you become a fish out of water at your job.

"A fish out of water is someone who is different than others around him. Because you don't blend in, you'll be heard when you speak out and take action. But you want to stand out in a positive way."

How do you do that? Well, I am glad you asked. With branding, of course! Again, here is my shameless plug.

I branded myself as "The Reinvention Guy" and you should do the same. No, don't become the "The Reinvention Guy." *Instead, discover what your mojo is... what really sets you apart from everyone else!*

Really... What Do YOU Bring to The Table?

Yes, it takes work. And as daunting as it may be, branding is not painful. (Unless you're a cow on a ranch.)

Here are a few questions to make your search for your own personal brand easier:

- Do you stand out or blend in as an employee?
- If you left your company tomorrow, would it grind to a halt or even notice your chair was empty?
- Do you come to work on time, early, or late? (More on this later.)
- Do you have a relationship with the person who can give you what you want? (That very special supervisor.)
- Do you know anything about his or her family? The names of his or her kids? Does he or she know anything about yours? (Yes, we call this schmoozing.)
- Do you really care about the company — or is it just a job with decent health benefits? (THIS is so important!)
- Do you spend any time or money learning new skills that can bring more value to your job? (Very important!)
- Do you have a plan for where you want to be in three years? In five? Ten?
- Does your boss even *know* you have a vision or that you're doing these other things, like taking courses to boost your knowledge and Contributing Value for the company? (If not, shouldn't they?)

I present these questions to you simply to get you thinking, so don't beat yourself up if you don't like the answers. Just change your behavior.

Now when your boss thinks of you, she'll be thinking, "Man, what a hard worker Jack is." Or "Susan's really dedicated. She was already here when I arrived this morning... and she was still here when I left."

And no, they will NOT think you have no life! Instead they'll probably think that your "brand" is that of a hard worker who is dedicated to solving the challenges of the projects you are given at the company.

Then guess what? **More times than not, down the road perhaps, you will get whatever you request just so your boss can keep you around!**

Of course, once you've "reinvented yourself" and made it to (drum roll please) Model Employee Status, it's time to start asking for what you want.

It's all In the Delivery!

As with anything else, there's a wrong way and a better way to do it.

The Wrong Way

"I want a raise now."

The Better Way

"I want a 10% raise over the next 30 days."

Being specific is a better tactic then just announcing you want a raise. You really do not want to just kick down your boss's door in a la *The Terminator* style and demand:

> YOU: (A la Governor Arnold) "Give me a raise or I must hurt you!"
> BOSS: "Johnson, I like your moxie... let me call payroll right now!"

Sorry to say, standing up to the boss and taking a take-no-prisoners stand like the above exchange usually only works in movies.

In this case, your boss will call security and hand you your walking papers instead. Now, I've never actually seen "walking papers," but I imagine they're a first cousin to the pink slip.

Remember, asking for what you want doesn't always mean asking for more moolah. Asking for what you want could include more flextime to spend with your kids, or taking a continuing education course. Whatever you want, just keep this vital guideline in mind:

Get Clear About What You Want

As mentioned earlier, during the course of your career, you might have a vague feeling of dissatisfaction about your job (that gnawing sense that there's something just not right) without knowing what that thing is.

Once more with gusto — get this clear and out in the open by asking yourself some questions. Things like:

- What part of your job gets you so jazzed that you can't wait to get up and go to work?
- On the other hand, what are the cons of the job that make you want to crawl into the fetal position and repeat to yourself, "Mommy, I don't feel well today...don't make me go to work!"
- Okay, you got news that a relative left you quite an inheritance. "Easy street here I come", you think. What part of your old job would you greatly miss? (i.e. perks, coworkers, etc.)

▌ Somehow you've gone back in time to an old job... what makes you thrilled to be back and why?

Research Your Options

Don't you love these little quizzes I give you?

Again, it's just like a relationship with the opposite sex. Once YOU know what you want, you'll need to figure out how to get those things without leaving your current employer.

For example, if you want to work flextime, maybe your company already offers it. Go to your HR department and ask.

"BUT Peter... I did! And they have no flextime!"

Then take action — if flextime isn't available, research it and build a case for it to present to your boss.

That's right, more home work. If you want something, then do your best to become a master persuader!

If you want to take a course, figure out how to present it to your boss in terms of how it will help him or her and the company as a whole. Think out of your cube. Simply list ways the course will help make you a better employee and an asset to your department.

Figure Out Who, When, and How to Ask

The 'who' is easy. Who can give you what you want?

Sometimes, though, we get hung up on the 'when' and 'how'. Should we e-mail them? Call them on the phone? Are mornings or afternoons better? What about Mondays?

Then you get more neurotic as you strategically plan "your mission" — timing is everything.

As I've noted above, your approach can be a huge determining factor in whether or not you get what you want, so do it right.

IDENTIFY ANY BARRIERS—THEN BUST THROUGH THEM, BABY!

This is the part where you need to climb inside your boss's head a little bit and think about what you want from their point of view.

I used to do this all the time when contemplating the best time to spring into action going after my goals at the company where I worked.

Every company has land mines... every company has their hoops to jump through. So consider these mine fields:

- Are they hampered by the company's policies and procedures?
- Are they worried that if they give you what you want, they'll have to do the same for everyone else in your division? (Are you going to upset the apple cart at work?)
- What's in it for them?

Yes, I know you are special. I know you bring a lot to the table. But what about your coworkers?

Consider what they will get as a result of you getting what you want, and consider it in those terms.

Yes, taking a course, changing job duties, or perhaps, joining Toastmasters will not only make you feel better, it'll make you a better employee, increase your productivity, and make you more valuable to your boss. But remember...

In life and in business there's a pecking order and everyone is doing the same dance — looking out for their own backsides!

Look at it this way. Your section's output will increase and your boss will look like a million bucks to her boss, and so on.

Once more, make a list of all the things in your company that will improve as a result of you getting whatever it is you want, and explain these things to your boss. Keep thinking like an entrepreneur.

NOW YOU'RE READY TO ASK

<u>Reinvention Guy's Take-Away Tip</u>: Of course, there's always the chance that the boss will say no! Well, what then? It happens. Being prepared for the possibility beforehand will help you turn it around. In the event your boss says, "No way, Jose," you can:

- Ask again in a different way or at a different time. Ask how you can help to make it work.
- Ask what is possible, if not this exact request.
- Ask when it might be possible.
- Ask what you can do so that it might be possible someday, and then shut up and listen.

● Never give up, recognize why you didn't succeed (at that moment), and have a Plan B to use later on.

Taking these steps can help you ask for and get what you want. Business and success guru and co-creator of the *Chicken Soup* for the Soul series, Jack Canfield says you have "nothing to lose and everything to gain by asking." (Sure, easy for him to say, he's sold over a zillion books and probably owns an Island somewhere in the South Pacific!)

But he's probably right. Don't you think? I mean, what's the worse that could happen? They could say no, and you don't get what you want?

Well, so what? You don't have what you want now, so what's changed? Think about it this way the next time you're afraid to ask for something you really want and need.

OKAY, NOW IT'S "THE BOSSES'" TURN!
Are you asking your key employees what makes them keep showing up for work every day, or how to keep them there? If not, why not?

Maybe you think it's illegal, or believe they'll tell you something you don't want to hear. Or possibly you're just afraid of putting the idea of jumping ship in someone's head (as if they weren't thinking about it already).

On the other hand, you might think that even if an employee does want to leave, you're powerless to stop them, so why bother? We live in a fast-pace world. That said, many managers are even pressed for time. And because they are, they might not take the time to ask their employees what makes them stay.

The Dangers of Not Asking

Why not just guess? You might be right some of the time. Throwing more money at them in the form of raises and bonuses will do in a pinch, but know this:

Buyer Beware: Money is never the only thing keeping your workers where they are.

What if what they really want is a chance to learn something new? To gain more visibility in the organization? To telecommute? You won't be able to guess these things, which means you have to ask your rank and file what they are going through!

Imagine all the positive outcomes of asking. Taking a real interest in your employees is just part of the equation for giving your staff respect! Asking the person what it'll take to make them stay makes them feel more valued and important. (Again, this can all be done without hugs.)

Caring + Loyalty = Retention

<u>Reinvention Guy's Take-Away Tip</u>: I can't stress enough that once you do what I outlined above, your staff will feel as if you care about them. They'll be more loyal to you and to the company. In fact, just the act of asking is, in itself, a great retention strategy.

Here are two things you can do right now to make sure you know why your people are staying, or wanting to go:

- **Think back to a time when you stayed with one company for a long period of time.** Ask yourself what kept you there? Write down two or three big reasons why you stayed as long as you did.
- **Ask each of your employees what keeps them at your company or in your department.** Make a card or note in your computer for every employee's answer. Once a month, review these notes and ask yourself what you've done for that employee that relates to their needs.

The point is, however you do it, you need to ask! And you won't really know for sure unless you do. Now, let's look at what it takes to get what you want out of your work.

IN REVIEW
To get what you want at work:

- Get clear and be specific on what you really want.
- Do your homework and figure out who, when, where, and how to ask.
- Identify and bust through any barriers that can keep you from reaching your goal.
- Never give up if you don't succeed at getting what you want at that moment and have a PLAN B in place to use down the line.

FOR THE BOSSES
- Think back to a time when you stayed at a company for a long time. What kept you there?
- Ask your employees what keeps them at your company or in your department.

I remember when I was very active in show business. Back then I blamed everything that was or was not happening to me, everything that was bothering me, on some outside force that was keeping me from my idea of fulfillment, which at the time was stardom!

You see, the real problem was that I was in complete denial of who was causing all this angst. Yep, you guessed it! *It was me.* I imagine by now you have a good idea where I am going with the next chapter, don't you? Then let's get to it, shall we?

"No Farnsworth, I'm not firing you. I'm enhancing your advancement opportunities."

CHAPTER 4:

You've Got to Give it to Get It

"Be nice to people on your way up because
you meet them on your way down."

—Jimmy Durante
(or said to Jimmy Durante by an elevator operator when they reached the lobby)

Remember the Tom Cruise movie, *Jerry McGuire*? One of the great taglines in that film, besides "You had me at hello", was when one of Jerry's clients kept saying, "Show me the money!"

But what did he do for that money?

He complained. That's right! All he did was bitch and moan about his teammates, his leaky roof, and other personal and financial problems.

Meanwhile, his coach thought he was too small for a wide receiver, and no one could stand his egotistical attitude when he was out on the field, blaming others for his poor performance during games.

He was excellent at the blame game. If he missed the ball, it was because another player threw it wrong, or because his fellow players and fans weren't giving him his "love." So let me be so blunt as to ask:

Are You a Prima Donna?

Does this sound like anyone you know? Most every industry and company has their prima donnas. Don't take this the wrong way, but are you that person for your company?

Do you constantly gripe and moan about your job duties? Your hours? Your low pay?

> "Why don't I move to India? On what they are paying me here, I could live like a King there."

Do you turn red in the face when someone else gets the promotion you knew you were destined to get?

"Frank? FRANK GOT MORE MONEY for doing what?! I was hired two days before he was, for crying out loud!"

Be honest. All of us at one time or another has come unglued when things didn't go our way at the office. It is, in fact, a good thing to vent on occasion.

In my former life, before I reinvented myself, I LIVED to complain. (When humorists complain, we are hired to find the humor in challenging situations. In essence, getting paid to bitch and moan.)

Back then, it was frustration that propelled me to blow off steam. And besides, when all you work is just forty-five minutes a night (on a stage making drunk people laugh), you have lots of time on your hands to complain.

But you know what? In the long run, it never made me happier and it certainly NEVER got me what I wanted, i.e. respect, more money, more opportunities, etc. It all boils down to this:

We seem to complain about things that we feel are NOT in our control!

Now, if you have taken the advice of Chapter One to heart and stopped blaming others (except your family, of course, but that's ANOTHER book), then good for you — you're halfway to reaching your goals!

But here's the bottom line. **If you want to reinvent yourself in your present position, you can't wait until you get a raise and** *then* **become a top performer.**

No one is going to promote an employee to get them to do what they are supposed to be doing in the first place. (Unless, of course, you work for a LARGE insurance company, whose name I won't mention, and you're given bonuses for sucking at what you do to begin with!)

What does this all mean to you? It means if you want to be a superstar at your work, start acting like one!

Of course, these days, everyone has excuses as to why they are not moving up the food chain at their job.

If could be office politics or a variety of reasons. As you know, nothing is perfect, and in any relationship there are ups and downs.

That being said, never let on to your boss that you do NOT like what you are doing, or that performing certain tasks is beneath you.

Common sense dictates you should always be a team player, and you should especially be one during a challenging economy where your boss can outsource your job to India.

That being said, workers still shoot themselves in the foot when their boss makes certain requests of them.

According to Karen Burn, author of *The Amazing Adventures of Working Girl: Real-Life Career Advice You Can Actually Use*, there are certain phrases one should eliminate from one's vernacular, especially if your boss makes a request of you.

1. **"This job is easy! Anyone could do it!"** It's the little things in life and at work that we have to be aware of. Imagine saying that this job is a no-brainer. Saying it the wrong way could very well tell your boss that the work you are doing is meaningless.

   Perhaps your boss did that exact job before he was promoted. See where I am going with this? Making statements like this could be taken the wrong way and puts down the whole company. If it's easy, then do it, and then move on to the next task quickly. You might say instead, "Hey, no problems... let me get to it!"

2. **"That's not my job."** Sure, that might have got a big laugh from Freddie Prinze on the old show *Chico and The Man*, but it won't cut it in the new workplace. If you're asked to do a certain task, instead of turning it down, you should investigate why your boss wants you do it.

   If you don't feel in your gut that you're up to the task, or it might not be beneficial to the company, ask someone else to do it.

3. **"It's not my fault."** Sure, you might say that to your mom when you break her vase fighting with your brother, but NOT in the workplace. Again, if there is a problem, fix it. If you did, in fact, screw up, own up to it and then come up with a solution — as quickly as you can.

4. **"It's not my problem."** Wrong thing to say when there is a crisis. If trouble is brewing you might want to pitch in and come up with a solution. If you don't, and don't have anything constructive to say, then silence is definitely golden during this time. Management and co-workers gravitate towards people that get things done and have the right attitude to persevere. But you knew that, right? Of course, you did!

5. **"I can only do one thing at a time."** Yes, I know we all get overwhelmed with requests, but learn to multi-task. Let's face it, snapping that you can't handle "the pressure", or don't like the job is saying to all within earshot that you are NOT up to the task.

6. **"It can't be done."** I worked at an office where the IT guy was like Scotty from Star Trek. Remember when Kirk always needed more power in the thrusters? Scotty would lament, "Captain, it just can't be done..."

Well, that is exactly what this IT guy said almost every time. Maybe he didn't want to be bothered. Or perhaps, it couldn't be done!

But one thing is for sure, he hardly ever came up with a solution. HINT: Even if the action being suggested is truly impossible, saying it is can make you look ineffective or incapable — even worse, it is telling your subconscious that you will not come up with a solution.

Search for ways to make it happen... and then *to boldly go where no man has gone before!* (No more Star Trek references, I promise!)

7. **"I am way overqualified for this job."** Hey, perhaps you are. Well, good for you, Sparky. But the fact is, this is the job you have. You agreed to take it on and, while you may now regret that decision, it's still your job. Complaining that it's beneath you only makes you look bad. Plus, coworkers doing similar jobs may resent and dislike you. And guess what? Bosses will not think, "Oh, this is a superior person whom I need to promote." Nope, they'll think, "What a jerk."

As you can probably surmise by now, your goal every day is to be a first class employee in every respect. Then, and only then, will you be able to ask for that raise or other job duties. Heck, you might not even have to ask!

Once again, it all comes down to respect.

Do you respect your bosses, your coworkers, your customers? Do you respect yourself enough to respect these people? (R-E-S-P-E-C-T just like the song says.)

Or do you find yourself rolling your eyes at these folks, or building a voodoo doll in their likeness when they are not around? (Pins optional.)

5 Ways to Get More Respect at Work!

1. Make sure you're a solid performer in everything you do. Top performers almost always get more respect.

2. Find out who *does* and who *doesn't* respect you, and figure out why. Ask a friend at work to give you their honest opinion about how much you're respected (or not) and why.

3. Tell the person who can give you what you want that you want and need more respect. Be specific about what type of respect you mean.

4. Figure out what changes you want to make in order to get more respect, and then make them today.

5. Give respect. Think about how and when you respect others. Treat others the way you want to be treated.

On occasion, old biases and leanings get in the way here. Your best bet is to get them out in the open. Do you have leanings that cause you to negatively judge people with different weight, skin color, political or religious views, age, or gender? (C'mon, we're human, we all have some flaws, don't we?)

If so, then how do these feelings affect your ability to give respect to others? Perhaps you talk to some people more than others, or avoid some altogether.

Naturally, this book is not to be a substitute for therapy. But I want you to investigate these problem areas. When I was an in-house copywriter and marketing consultant for a company, my goal in having fun in the workplace was to find out what made certain coworkers laugh.

Humor is the closest connection between two people. Make someone laugh and you've connected on a visceral level with them. In a positive way, you are hitting their hot buttons. Once I discovered what made certain coworkers laugh, I knew I could relate to them on another, different level.

For example, no matter how crappy a day he was having, I always knew what to do to make Ben, the graphic designer, laugh. In turn, my co-workers would go out of their way to bust my chops, but in a good way.

Andrew and Mike would both razz me and I'd say to them,

> "Look at you both... you had all day to come up with that remark and it fizzled like a weak scud missile. How pathetic."

Then we'd all break out laughing at their feeble attempts at humor.

Naturally, I could on and on about humor in the workplace, but will save that for another book.

Have Negative Feelings? Here's How to Handle it!

Now, whenever you encounter possible negative leanings (and you know what I am talking about), **decide right there and then, to reinvent yourself and make a change. It takes work.**

I realized in BR (Before Reinvention) that I had a few character flaws that got in my way and were holding me back from reaching certain business goals I wanted to attain.

Having them followed me around for a good part of my early career. No one ever really told me what was holding me back, but instinctively, I had a strong idea.

During the comedy boom, as funny as I was, I had a rep for being a "nudge."

Unfortunately, I didn't attract the work that should have come my way. Instead, I went after it like a jaguar goes after a gazelle. If a booker told me to call them back for an engagement on a certain day, I would — relentlessly.

But I had no choice. If I wanted to pay my rent, I had to be a pain to get the gig. Instead of attracting agents and bookers to get me work, I would do the opposite and turn them off.

I went after what I wanted, damn the consequences or who got in my way. (Unfortunately, it turned many a comedic brethren off and at times sabotaged my career.)

Yes, being motivated and going after your dream is one thing, but crossing the line is another.

The First Step to Ridding Yourself of a Flaw is to Acknowledge You Have One!

What was holding me back along my journey was the *desperation* of wanting something too badly. Others can sense that. Oh, boy, can they sense that! I swore in my new career that once I reinvented myself, I would do my best to get rid of it (the desperation)!

Sure, I would still have tenacity, but I would pull back more, give people a chance to get to know me, and not be a jackhammer in trying to land engagements.

But enough about me, let's get back to you. What is that little flaw that is holding you back? Is it that part of you that immediately makes a judgment about someone, so you avoid them?

Want a quick and painless way to correct it? Just do the opposite. Try appreciating the people you are avoiding and see where they are coming from.

Dr. Todd Kashdan, a clinical psychologist and professor of psychology at George Mason University, says lack of curiosity is a breeding ground for stereotyping and discrimination, ignorance, rigid conformity, inflated confidence, and dogmatism.

Make a change! You never know, you just might discover that you have more in common with them than you thought possible.

FOR THE BOSSES

All right, bosses. Success, as *they* say, is a two-way street. (Note: To this day I still don't know who they are — but apparently *they* are very important.)

So, are you giving your fair share?

By that I mean, if someone asked your employees what kind of boss you are, what would they say?

1. Would they say that you are friendly, hard-working, and dedicated?
2. Would they say that you are easy to work with?
3. Would they say you're completely mercurial, fly off the handle, an unpredictable despot? (Yes, that was the last man I worked for... and surprisingly, I liked the whacko!)

Employees will put up with a wide range of behaviors from you, just as you do from them. But one thing they won't put up with for long is disrespect!

I know some of this might be common sense and you've heard this all before. Just as they have to earn your respect, you must earn theirs. That means treating them as you want to be treated.

Go through the list of differences above and see if you have any preconceived notions about any of them.

- What assumptions have you made about your employees that fit under these categories?
- Do you feel differently about some of them now that you've gotten to know them better?

No matter how unprejudiced we think we are, everyone has some conception of people who are different from ourselves.

It's human nature to make general assumptions about a person's behavior, and then assign that behavior to a group the person belongs to!

Believe it or not, these things were learned, and you must unlearn them if you are to manage your people effectively.

GETTING IN THE MOOD

What does this all mean? It means treating everyone with respect, and it means controlling your moods and cutting back on chocolate and Red Bull. Have you ever worked with someone prone to wild mood swings? Could your employees say that about you?

Here are three things you can do to control your mood:

- **Notice your mood swings and take control.** Go off by yourself while you work through your problems. (Have your own personal "time out.")
- **If you go off on someone, apologize.** As much as you may think the opposite, apologizing isn't a sign of weakness on your part. In reality, it's a sign of respect.
- **If you are having serious emotional issues**, get help from a counselor.

THE INVISIBLE EMPLOYEE

There's this great episode of the 1980's *Twilight Zone* television series where a guy was sentenced to be invisible for one year. A mark was put on his forehead and no one was allowed to speak to him or acknowledge he existed. (I know families that do this to each other!) Naturally, he went crazy within a short period of time.

Are you treating any of your employees in this fashion? Could you be disrespecting your staff by NOT acknowledging these people at all? Doing so makes them feel unknown, unappreciated, and just plain unloved.

Worse, your employees will feel like their contributions to the organization aren't important. And sure enough, loyalty is gone and they'll eventually look elsewhere for the attention and approval they seek.

Yes, it sounds like petulant children with special needs. But they're not. They're the grease that keeps the engine of your company running.

Here's what you can do to "see" the invisible employee:

- **This may sound like a no-brainer, but it truly is the little things you do that get noticed by your employees.** One of the most important things you can do is to say hello to them as you walk down the hall, or past their office or cubicle.
- **Regardless of the size of your company, try your best to actually learn and address your employees by their first names.** As Dale Carnegie always says, "everyone loves the sound of their own name." My former boss was actually a great guy, quite gregarious, but so wrapped up in multi-tasking that he sometimes forgot to say hello to his employees as he was walking down the hall past their offices.
- **Smile at them, shake their hands, and introduce them to others, even if those others are people of a higher rank.** I guarantee you they will not feel invisible after that.

■ **Surprise your employees.** Do things out of the ordinary. I have an assistant that I am working with now who is handling a lot of tasks and assignments for me. She recently sent me an invoice for services done.

Guess what? I gave her a bonus even after she said I didn't have to. Surprised, she sent me a heartfelt thank you telling me her clients never do what I did ... and that they could learn something from me about how to treat staff. (Oh, and I also always pay her immediately, thank you very much.)

Think my assistant isn't going to go the extra yard for me now?

What I explained to my new VA (Virtual assistant) is that when certain legs of my business reach their financial goals, she will be rewarded along with my success. Do you think this woman has an incentive to make our business arrangement work?

TRUST

Do you trust your employees? (Or do you wait for them to show you that they can be trusted before you trust them?)

> *The bottom line is when you trust your employees,*
> *most of them will be worthy of that trust.*

They won't want to let you down, so they instantly become better people. The trustworthy people will practically fall all over themselves to prove their trustworthiness to you.

Act like you don't trust them and watch what happens. You'll both become paranoid. They'll start looking over their shoulders every five minutes to make sure you aren't watching them, and you'll catch them doing it, which makes you think they're guilty of something.

It'll be like a horror movie. All of sudden the theme song from Jaws will start to play in the background. You'll hear your name mentioned in hurried whispers and think you are being talked about negatively. Which, of course, you will be. Why? (Beat) Because you don't trust your people!

If, by any slim chance, you are in this situation, here are a couple of things you can do:

■ **Evaluate your trust issues.** Do you believe trust is a gift or need evidence of trustworthiness before you bestow it?

■ **Just trust your employees.** Tell them you trust them and act like you trust them. Give them responsibilities and let them carry them out without any micromanaging from you.

All's Fair in Love and Work

<u>Reinvention Guy's Take-Away Tip:</u> If your employees perceive that they are being treated unfairly, then THIS will happen — they will walk. Unfairness is the same as disrespect to many of them.

- Really examine how you communicate with your staff.
- Think about how they view your decisions and the changes you make.
- Do you respect and implement their ideas?
- Do you value their input? If not, sooner or later, you will lose them.

And then all the energy and training you put into them will be for naught! In marketing, it takes a certain amount of time and money to get a new customer. It is far easier to market to a present customer than it is to find a new one. The same idea can be applied to keeping your staff!

As you can plainly see, there's nothing really difficult about treating your employees with respect. *The secret is simply to treat them the same way you want to be treated.*

IN REVIEW

- Make sure you're a solid performer in everything you do.
- Figure out who does and who doesn't respect you, and figure out why.
- Tell the person who can give you what you want that you want and need more respect.
- Discover what changes you want to make in order to get more respect, and then make them today.
- Give respect. Simply, treat others the way you want to be treated.

FOR THE BOSSES

- Do try (as best you can) to control your moods.
- Notice your employees by greeting them, calling them by name, and introducing them to your colleagues.
- Trust your employees, and they will return that trust.
- Look at how you communicate with your employees.

Whew! Controlling moods... trusting employees... communicating with employees... respect... This certainly ain't your "granddad's job", is it?!

Well, it's time to climb off my soapbox now as we head off into Chapter 5 and consider the most efficient ways to reach your lofty goal of reinventing yourself in the workplace.

A Middle Manager Stands at the Pearly Gates.

Got Goals?

"Even if you are on the right track, you will get run over if you just sit there."

—Will Rogers

Now that we've done some personal evaluation and learned how to ask for what we want, it's time to sit down and create some goals. Now you lament to yourself,

"YAY! More homework!"

No worries, but if your head is nodding and your eyes are starting to glaze over, just bear with me.

And that's because goal setting is a very important process. One that all successful people have used to become... uh, well... successful. Going through life without a plan is like driving from New York to Los Angeles without a GPS.

Sure, you can do it, but you'll arrive late, broke, and exhausted. (And no, in case you are wondering, I NEVER arrived from New York to Los Angeles — late!)

You see, having a plan means you'll know exactly what to do and when to do it. It means not having to guess. It means not taking on things in your life that will not elevate you to where you want to be. So let's get this party started.

SEEK CONTENTMENT

The first stop on your path to setting goals is to seek contentment. Ahh, yes! The Big C in life. Seeking contentment in all you do will not only help you be, well...uh... content, in addition, it can't help but keep you in line with your values.

If you remember in previous chapters, we outlined our beliefs about work, as well as our interests and strengths. We did this so you would know what type of work makes you truly happy.

Remember: Keeping these preferences in mind will make it easier to make and then stick to your long and short term goals.

STICK TO YOUR VALUES

I hope you will agree that we all have values that dictate our career, lifestyle, and family life. For better or worse, they are our filter for processing everything that comes at us, whether we're at work or at home. They are the perennial moral compass that helps us make important decisions.

When we really know deep down what our values are, we make decisions more clearly and consistently, and then hopefully, we're going to make the right ones.

Therefore, we cannot really be truly happy unless our decisions and goals are consistent with our core values.

An example in my case was when I was an in-house copywriter for a health and financial information publisher. This firm had clients that came to my boss to hire our company to do I.R.'s. These are financial direct mail letters that heavily promote a penny stock so it skyrockets its price.

Then once it hits a specific higher price, insiders dump the stock. They make out like bandits and the little guy gets hammered. They are aptly called "pump and dumps".

Sure, there is small print on the advertisement that relinquishes the publisher from any culpability in the very likely event you lose your investment (and you will). In case you're wondering, legally, my boss was NOT held accountable. Morally, it's a different story.

Because I believe in karma, I refused to promote that product because of my values! Once again with gusto, class. It all boils down to balance. This goes back to having the little devil on one shoulder and the little angel on the other. Both are trying to persuade you.

Yes, we change as we get older, and with it, our values can also change during our journey. So, every once in a while you need to reacquaint yourselves with them, especially as they relate to your current working environment. The plain truth is...

If you find your work is not compatible with your values,
it's time to make a change.

So ask yourself right now: Is your work life/career compatible with your values? Maybe you've always dreamed of working for environmental causes, but you took a job, heaven forbid, with Big Oil, for instance. You're devoted to your family. But your corporation's culture values ten hour days and 90 hour work weeks.

I think you know where I'm going with this. No job is perfect. No environment is perfect. But remember what YOU are all about. The job and your career may pay really well, but if your values are not compatible with other areas of your life, well then…

Houston, We Got a Problem!

(Obi Wan Kenobi) "Listen to Your Inner Voice, Luke."

No, NOT that one! Not "The Voice" that says you are going to fail at everything you try, that you're not good enough, and that you're better off NOT rocking the proverbial boat at your job. (Please get MY father's voice out of your head, now!)

No, my reinventor, I am talking about the other inner voice. The positive one that tells you everything is going to be all right and that you can reach any goals you set for yourself. (Ahhh! Cue up angelic-like music.)

JUST SET BIG GOALS

No tiny, little, easy to obtain goals will do it. You've got to set big goals. I call them Monster Goals.

No pain, no gain. Listen, if we set goals that are too easy to obtain, we don't challenge ourselves and thus break out of our comfort zones. We end up setting goals that only improve our lives instead of transforming them.

The way I see it, you wouldn't be reading this book if you didn't want a dramatic change, right?

Rebooting your career means making a major shift in your working life. The truth is, you can't do that without setting some major, monster goals.

So how do we accomplish that? Well, a good monster goal should be specific and measurable.

SPECIFIC

Monster goals are not vague; they're ultra specific. For instance…

Goal: "I will lose weight"

> Nahhh, too vague! Try this goal on for size:

> "I will lose 70 pounds and get my own reality show detailing my success!"

Ahhh, you see? Much better. You've given yourself a specific amount of weight to lose.

Although the dream of getting your own reality show might be out of your grasp. Wait, on second thought, the way Hollywood works these days, you might just get one!

Meanwhile, this is a good start. But how do we make this goal really powerful? Read on.

MEASURABLE

If your goal isn't measurable in some way, you'll reach your deadline with only the vaguest sense that you actually completed it. Let's revisit our weight loss goal above and make it measurable:

"Come hell or high water, I will lose 40 pounds by December 31st, (fill in the year)!"

Wouldn't you be more likely to meet a goal like this, than some vague goal with no time limit? Specificity is better... specificity gets the heart pumping and the adrenaline flowing.

Years earlier, my big goal was to learn persuasive copywriting, so I could earn a six figure income — by a specific date! I focused like a laser on THAT goal. Nothing was going to stop me from reaching it. And I did it a lot sooner—than later! (We pause as author pats himself on the back.)

BRAINSTORM SOME GOALS

Now that you know what elements make a good goal, start a list. Go crazy.

Don't censure anything that comes to mind (for now). Remember, at this point in the game, no goal is too outrageous. Want to be President of the company? Great! Write it down. Want to make six figures in sales commissions this year? Put it on the list, baby!

Hey! You make a shopping list when you go to a grocer, right? Then do the same thing with your life! Put it down... once reached, check it off. (Oh, and don't forget to pick up eggs.)

Spend some time on this list, and really come up with a big list of goals. Use broad categories like Personal, Work, Relationships, and Financial.

Come up with goals for each heading. Keep working at it until you've hit all the major areas and issues in your life. Also, make sure you come up with short, medium, and long-term goals. To do this, ask yourself, "Self, where would you like to be in a year?"

It's The Journey... NOT the Destination
(Bull! It's the destination, and you know it!)

<u>Reinvention Guy's Take-Away Tip</u>: For medium-term goals, ask yourself where you want to be about three years from now. For long-term goals, ask yourself where you want to be in five years.

Is there a method to this madness? Yes, doing this will help you create deadlines for each of your major goals and let you evaluate them further down the road.

Once you've finished your list, measure your prospective goals against your lifelong interests.

Do these ideas match areas in which you enjoy spending your time? If one of your goals is to become a star salesperson, but you hate selling, then common sense dictates that being in sales is not for you.

NEXT, MEASURE YOUR IDEAS AGAINST YOUR STRENGTHS
- Is this an area that you have shown an aptitude for?
- If not, do you feel you could develop the skills you would need?
- Can you see yourself succeeding at this and being happy? If so, go for it.

Now, it's time to decide how your current working environment would affect these ideas. Is your employer the right culture for you? Will they allow you to accomplish these objectives? If not, what type of culture do you need to be successful?

Now, look at your values. Are these new goals in line with them? No matter how you try, you will not get very far with goals that are in opposition to your values.

One more time with gusto: *When your values are in line with your goals, you create a synergy that will propel you farther than you thought you could make it on your own.*

In no time, you will be living a life that you'll love, one that you mapped out from day one. This will give you an overall feeling of pride and accomplishment. You'll breathe a deep sigh of relief and say to yourself, "Life is good at the top."

IN REVIEW
To set goals:
- Dig deep and seek contentment every day you are working.
- Stick to your values.
- Listen to your inner voice.
- Set monster goals that are specific and measurable and challenge you as a person.
- Make a huge list of goals under different areas of your life such as Personal, Career, Relationships, and Financial.

Are you interested in NOT taking the scenic route to success, and instead, reaching those wondrous goals FASTER? Well, Chapter 6 reveals a proven strategy that should help put you on the right path sooner.

"McWit, I'm going to make you more efficient ...
no matter how much it slows you down."

Model Your Way to Success

*"You must learn from the mistakes of others.
You can't possibly live long enough to make them all yourself."*

— Sam Levenson
(dead humorist, writer, and television host)

E veryone who has ever been successful at anything (whether it is business, sports, relationships, or anything else), have all done this one task that was critical to that success. It doesn't cost anything but your time. It's definitely proactive and all the greats have done it.

Trust me here. If you do this one thing, you could easily make leaps and bounds with your own career.

If you have an immediate department supervisor, the company owner, a coworker, a top salesperson, or a colleague in another department whose success you admire... don't admire them. Join them.

Notice What Others Are Doing And Copy Their Success In The Way That Works Best For You

Look at what they do, examine as best you can how they approach their job, challenges, and the solutions they come up with. Guess what? You will be surprised at how they may not be any better than you.

I've done this during my reinvention, and I am constantly doing it in regards to being a better copywriter and speaker. And especially when it comes to being a more effective marketer. The learning never stops. When a marketer created a new model for say, lead generation (getting folks interested in my products), I investigated what they were doing right.

I realized that the person I was modeling after was no smarter or motivated than I was. He or she just figured it out faster.

And it's the same with you. The folks who are getting things done and having breakthroughs are really no more talented or intelligent than you are.

Why are they where they are, and you are where you are? Luck, perhaps... but mostly, they have taken certain steps to get to where they are.

Again, in the marketing world this is done all the time. For instance, a client of mine wants to create a new product and then market to his list. He doesn't know if it'll be a hit, and he certainly doesn't want to blow a wad of cash and fail in the process.

Sure, he could try, for pennies on the dollar, testing it on-line, and many do. But another more sure-fire way is to see what is already working in the market place. My client accomplished this task by watching his competitors like hawks!

You see, a lot of times, a smart marketer wants to go with what is truly a winner and not reinvent the wheel.

A smart marketer/entrepreneur watches his competition to see what offers are appearing again and again in the mail. In reality, a "smart marketer" is doing his research while his competitor is doing the heavy lifting for him.

Again, if a certain sales promotion appears in his mailbox a lot (let's say every few weeks), that direct mail marketer knows that that particular sales promotion is a winner. Why? Simply because a prudent marketer (his competitor) will NOT keep mailing an offer that's losing him money.

Remember when a stream of infomercials was over-selling the notion that anyone can have ROCK-SOLID ABS in just two minutes a day without dieting? (Yeah, right!) It was like the invasion of the Ab Machines for a while.

Why? Simply because these companies were reading the market and delivering on what people wanted!

Here's a marketing tip: You will always reach your goals faster when you give people what they want... NOT what they need! People don't need chocolate, but they want it! See?

This is how a direct marketer stays in business. Giving people what they want. To accomplish this task the direct marketer does a small test first. If he breaks even on the promotion, then he knows he has a winner on his hands.

He then rolls out more direct mail pieces and rakes in the dough. (Hopefully after expenses are paid.)

You might think, "Well, aren't the two companies selling the same product then?" Yes, and no. It's the same product, but the other marketer makes significant changes

REBOOT YOUR CAREER   27 Ways to Reinvent Yourself in the Workplace …

to his product or service and comes up with a **USP** (Unique Selling Proposition) for it. (Remember when we discussed USP's earlier in this book?)

Well, you can model the success of others who have come before you. Again, if you can, and they're willing, meet with those people whose career at work you admire and discover how they reached that plateau.

Pick their brains in an easy-going way and see if you can do your best to model their success. Then figure out a way to tweak some of the steps they've taken to suit your needs.

Here's a terrific story that illustrates this point.

DAVID'S STORY

David Neagle is a business coach and consultant who teaches people how to use the law of attraction to achieve whatever they want. He makes millions every year showing people the same steps he used to become a success.

But here's the thing, he wasn't always such a success.

A high school dropout, David started out working as a forklift operator for a shipping company, spending long, terrible hours on a cold loading dock and cursing his existence.

On one particularly cold evening around 2am, David had an epiphany. A little voice inside his head said, "Change your attitude."

David set out that very instant to do just that. And he immediately started thinking about the most successful person he knew at that time, which was the owner of the company, and decided he would do what that guy does.

He noticed that his boss was always kind and courteous to everyone when he came by, treating everyone with the utmost respect. David started following his example.

He also started caring more about his work. Before, David was all about doing as little as he could get away with and then going home, not caring if the boxes he was loading were loaded properly, or fell over and got crushed. **Now, he took extra care to do everything right, even if he had to do it over.**

David's new attitude paid off, and within a few months he received a promotion usually reserved only for one of the owner's relatives at this small, family-owned company.

❖ 84 ❖

David's coworkers joked that he must be the boss's illegitimate nephew in order to get all this attention, but he didn't care. He just kept right on succeeding.

Today, David Neagle is a huge success. All because of a little epiphany he had years ago on a cold loading dock in the dead of night.

Now, maybe you're much better off than David was at that time. (Or maybe you've even got it worse.) But I hope you'll agree, you can learn a thing or three from this example.

Once again, simply find someone successful in your company or industry and objectively think about what got them there. Know that they didn't all get to the top by kissing the boss's behind!

▌ Examine their work habits.
▌ Do they consistently come in early and stay late?
▌ Do they constantly improve their skills?
▌ Do they interact with supervisors and coworkers in a friendly way?

Write down what they do and pick up their good habits.

Build Your Team of Supporters!

Here's some more good news. You don't have to play copycat with someone from afar. You can also get personal, one-on-one advice from someone who has been where you are and achieved great success. I'm talking about getting a mentor.

I have had quite a few mentors, or gurus, in my life. I looked closely at what they did and just modeled their behavior. Of course, some of these gurus were tough on me and I considered them "tormentors." Either way, I still got results.

Most of all, when gaining new skills, do it because you want to do it. Do it to gain that knowledge, not because you want to earn money at your job.

HOW TO FIND A MENTOR

You can take the advice above one step further by developing a one-on-one relationship with someone in your industry or organization who can help you be "all you can be!"

A mentor can cut the learning curve in mastering a skill by quite a bit. He (or she) can use their own experiences to help you avoid costly, time-wasting mistakes and get up the ladder much faster than you could on your own.

So, how do you find a mentor a.k.a. "The Wizard" to help you reach your goals?

Well, for starters, it helps if you know what to look for in one. Basically, a good mentor should be:

■ Able to help you increase your ability to reach your goals.
■ Able to teach you a new skill.
■ A good listener and able to provide you with constructive criticism.
■ Hook you up with the people you need to know to get ahead; someone who can include you in activities that will give you access to these people.
■ Give you the lowdown on the politics and power in your organization or industry.

So to start, just ask yourself, "What do I need?" Here is where you must really be honest with yourself and examine what skills you want, need to learn, or need to improve upon.

Once you do that, you should seek out the appropriate person to teach those skills. Here are some aspects of the search you should concern yourself with:

■ Do you want to learn from someone similar to, or different from, yourself?
■ Do you want someone from a similar background who came up the same way you did, or does it matter if they came by a different road?
■ Do you want to be mentored by someone you know, or do you want to find someone you've never met before?

Finally, you need to really decide how much time you want to spend on the process. Remember, time is a commodity that once spent you will never get back! So choose wisely, young Skywalker!

Alright, you have brainstormed with yourself and decided what kind of mentor you want. Now, it's time to find one.

Believe it or not, you can look for a mentor in your own department or another. And no, they do NOT have to be senior members of your firm. (A mentor can actually be older or younger, above you, or beside you in rank.)

My recommendation? Find someone who retired from your field recently, to avoid presenting a conflict of interest within your department (or at a competing firm). Below are a few tips to help you find your own Jedi Master.

Do Your Due Diligence!
(That's just a fancy phrase meaning research!)

One quick way to find "The One" is go on-line. Thanks to Al Gore, you can cyber search your coach.

All you do is simply research the names and backgrounds of people who have been successful in your area of interest.

They can be found by reading industry magazines, asking members of trade associations, attending trade shows and conventions, and yes, asking your colleagues for suggestions.

Keep your eyes and ears open. A good mentor could be lurking anywhere. That said, Michael Masterson has some great advice for finding yours:

> "Make a list of five successful business leaders in your industry who have retired within the last two to five years. Timeframe is important. If they've been out of the game longer than five years, they will be out of touch with changes that took place after they left. Any sooner, and they're not yet bored enough with retirement to start thinking about 'the good old days.'

> "Write each of them a short letter expressing your genuine admiration for their careers. List a few specific accomplishments, and then ask for advice on your career. Offer to buy them lunch, or if they live out of state, ask for a 15-minute phone call."

The odds are good that at least one of the five will respond favorably to your request for help. And if the two of you get along, congratulations, you just found yourself a mentor.

<u>Reinvention Guy's Take-Away Tip</u>: Whatever you do, don't mention money, at least, not at the outset. You'll likely find that many of the people you talk to are big believers in paying it forward and will offer you a little of their time for free. Just don't monopolize all of their time. Moreover, make sure you ask them what *you* can do for *them*.

TAKE ACTION ON THEIR ADVICE
This one seems like a no-brainer, but the reason most people don't succeed is because they fail to follow through on all the great advice that's out there.

Nothing is more disrespectful of a mentor's time than for their "mentee" to ignore their hard-won advice. **Listen, ask questions, listen some more, and then** *follow* **their example as closely as you can.**

GET MULTIPLE MENTORS
There is also no law that says you can't have more than one mentor. Just as Luke Skywalker had Obi Wan Kenobi and Yoda, you, too, can have more than one.

In fact, in today's fast-paced world, one-on-one mentoring relationships that stretch on for years are rare. It's more common to have multiple mentors who each teach you a different skill set. Once you've learned what you came to them to learn, you simply move on to another mentor who can teach you something else, and so on.

I call this "moving up" the mentor tree!

START YOUR OWN MASTERMIND GROUP

Ready to take it to another level and get LOTS of feedback? Well, you can do this by forming your own mastermind group.

> "Fantastic!!" you think, "A mastermind group... that's what I need! (beat) What's a mastermind group?"

Well, the definition of a mastermind group is:

> "... a group of likeminded people who all want to achieve the same goal, whether it's starting a business or rebooting their careers."

Mastermind groups have been used by some of the most successful business men in history, from Andrew Carnegie to Dale Carnegie.

It can be a gathering of people you've met online with similar goals, or a collection of your fellow disgruntled employees. It's best your meetings are not taken up with thinking of new ways to get back at your boss, a la Dabney Coleman and Dolly Parton in the movie 9 to 5.

The cool part of being in a mastermind group is it's sort of like having your own Jedi Council to do your bidding. **Its purpose, besides networking with other like-minded people, is to act as a sounding board for everyone's ideas and to share resources.**

> "Well, Reinvention Guy, if you're so smart, how do you start one?"

Great question. I am glad I asked. For guidance, I'm turning to mastermind group expert, Bill Hibbler. He is the co-author, along with business guru Joe Vitale, of the book *Meet and Grow Rich* (www.meetandgrowrich.com), and he has some great tips for forming your very own mastermind group.

▌**Keep it to 5-6 members.** More than that, and meetings can drag on too long. Less, and nothing gets done when one or two folks can't make it.

▌**Meet weekly or monthly.** You want to keep the momentum going within the group.

▋**Meet in a quiet, comfy place.** This way people won't mind sitting for two or three hours.

▋**Start out by seeking one person.** Keep adding members until you have your five.

I am a member of the *National Speakers Association* and the *Florida Speakers Association.* We are like-minded entrepreneurs who support each other in furthering the education and careers of speakers.

In whole, they are all pretty grounded people who want to see each of their members succeed. Yes, there are different levels of expertise, but for the most part, there are loads of speakers who are quite successful and pass their knowledge onto other members.

And this is an important point — in joining your own mastermind group, YOU want to align yourself with people who are at YOUR success level, or greater. In addition, these people should have skills and knowledge you don't have and vice versa. This way everyone benefits from each other!

Believe it or not, Anthony Robbins is in a mastermind group... with billionaires. Yes, even Anthony wants to learn and get to the next level of achievement. No doubt these billionaires want to share their money-making ideas with Tony, and they, I am sure, get quite a few self-improvement ideas from him.

GET YOURSELF A COACH

Now, if you're willing to spend some money, getting a professional coach is a very proactive idea, too.

Everyone has a coach nowadays, even other coaches. So what does this mean for you? It means if you're feeling stuck with no way out (can't find a mentor), and no one is giving you any honest, intelligent answers to your particular career problems, a good coach could deliver a good return on your investment.

Believe it or not, there are coaches for just about everything you can imagine. Like Baskin-Robbins, they come in many flavors: career change coaches, coaches for entrepreneurs, and even six-figure executive coaches. It's a regular "coachfest"! Do an Internet search for career coaches and you will see what I mean!

Allegedly, Bill Clinton had the Uber Coach, Anthony Robbins, assist him with blocks he was having.

Word of caution, finding a mentor or Mastermind Group is a lot like dating the right girl. And by that I mean, don't rush into anything! You want it to be a good fit with your values, wants, and needs. Keep looking until you find exactly what you need. Many of the guidelines for hunting a mentor also apply here.

If you meet your coach for a meet-and-greet, let's say at Starbucks, and the coach gets out of a 1989 Ford Fiesta, perhaps THAT coach isn't the right one for you!

Like a bad blind date that shows up looking nothing like her photo, your best bet is to hightail it to the next exit. Go home, nurse your wounds, do another Google search, or go to on-line forums and ask for recommendations! Networking with other like-minded folks at specialized events can also lead you to the right mastermind group.

Again, your goal is to find a coach who specializes in your field and has a proven track record of success.

If you are satisfied with their way of coaching and their background, make sure they are legit, and successful, and specialize in working with people just like you.

Another good vetting process is to talk to other clients, or otherwise reading testimonials from industry pros will give you a heads up. Oh, and ask your coach if you can talk to some of their clients. If they hesitate, then buyer beware!

FOR THE BOSSES

Okay, bosses, CEO's, Head Honchos … it's your turn once again. And by now, some of you are probably saying,

> "Ah, mentor schmentor. I never had a mentor, and I came up just fine. What are you whining about, Fogel!"

Well, just in case you've become too complacent about the happiness of your immediate underlings, let me reveal to you the price of doing nothing.

News Flash! This just in: According to data from the 1999 Emerging Workforce Study, 35 percent of employees who don't receive regular mentoring, plan to look for another job within 12 months, while just 16 percent of those with mentors expect to leave.

Yikes! Now there's a splash of cold water on the face. My advice? Take this mentoring thing seriously. I have gotten guidance from different mentors over the years, and I know other successful people from all walks of life use mentors.

There are Peak Performance mentors and coaches like Tom McCarthy (www.tommcarthy.com), who coach CEO's and top professional athletes.

According to experts, it takes around 1000 hours to master a new skill. With a mentor, someone who has reached the pinnacle of success within a particular niche guiding you, you can literally cut that time in half.

Here's the good news if you're a manager or CEO. You don't have to worry about your valued players sneaking off to see some secret Guru-On-The-Mount! Why? *Because you can, in fact, be a mentor yourself.* That's right, just eliminate the middle man, as they say.

And get this, what employees seek in a mentor are the same things they want from a caring manager.

That said, here are a few things you can do right now in order to act like a mentor to your employees:
- **Be a Model:** Be aware of your own behaviors, and point out others who would make good role models for your team.
- **Support** your employees for taking risks necessary to their growth.
- **Get acquainted** with your people, their skills and abilities, and help them make the most of their talents.
- **Tell it like it is** at your company. Help them avoid the pitfalls and office politics, the "unwritten rules" of your organization that don't appear in any manual, but are just as important as those that are.

An Ounce of Encouragement is Worth a Pound of Cure

Like the proverbial "he said, she said", managers and employees often disagree when the subject of encouragement comes up.

The employee will say, "She never encouraged me", while the manager will say, "I encouraged him all the time."

So, how can you effectively encourage, and therefore, keep your employees?

Well, one of the best ways to encourage is through your everyday interactions and conversations with your employees. I think you know the answer, but to review it, here are three ways right off the bat to do it:

- Notice some positive behavior of your employees.
- Say something good about it.
- Do something to encourage your employees' development.

Let's imagine your employee comes to you after playing with Excel with a new spreadsheet he's designed. Congratulate him, and ask him if he likes doing stuff like that, and find out if he'd like to do more.

See how this works? This type of "mentoring" (which comes off as nurturing, as well), is even more important if your time to sit down with employees is limited.

Experience has shown me it's the little things you do that reap big rewards! For many employees, a little of this kind of attention is all it takes to keep them from cruising the online job boards on their lunch breaks.

This works in the "real world" of business. But not in my old profession.

When I was performing in Florida, I would have killer shows with my buying agent present — not my personal agent who works on my behalf, but the agent who purchases my services for her client. Their job is to service the client and themselves, NOT the talent!

Anyway, this agent would never compliment me, no matter how well I did, or if I got a standing ovation.

Why? Because she didn't want to give me any ammo to use against her the next time she hired me and I asked for a raise. Her goal in dealing with talent is for moi "to do just okay" so the client doesn't complain. They say, "Love is never having to say you are sorry."

Well, in show business, giving a great performance means never having to compliment the performer, so he WON'T ask for more money!

Of course, I was an independent contractor and had many buyers of my talent, so if I didn't want to deal with an agent, I didn't have to.

In your case, dealing with your employee, the congratulating and positive reinforcement will go a long way to keep them happy. But I am sure you know this already, don't you? You savvy business person!

NURTURING ON THE FLY
Contrary to what you might believe, mentoring doesn't take a lot of time. Mostly it just takes a willingness to show another person that you care about them and want them to succeed.

Follow me as I digress once again for a moment. When I was in show business full-time, I never really had any mentors in my first profession. It was the School of Hard Knocks. Every man for himself.

In my second profession, copywriting and Internet marketing, I had quite a few mentors help me succeed. (And now back to our regularly scheduled reading.)

Pssst! Here's a secret! Nurture your employees' ideas when they come to you with suggestions, instead of initially shooting them down!

Take care of employee relationships by getting to know your workers and giving them an opportunity to get to know you.

It won't cost you a thing but a few minutes here and there, and what you'll be getting back is a motivated, happy employee who sticks around — priceless.

<u>Reinvention Guy's Take-Away Tip</u>: Show your employees the ropes at your company. C'mon, everyone has stories about the otherwise brilliant employee who didn't fit in and kept rubbing people the wrong way. As you know, these days, brilliance alone won't cut it in the competitive corporate world.

That's why you owe it to yourself, your company, and your employees to clue them in to things they may be doing that are irritating their coworkers, other supervisors, and especially yourself.

Take the time to give them the inside scoop. Tell them about the "unwritten rules" of your corporation's culture, the little things you won't find in a policy manual, but are just as important!

Why? Because everyone LOVES secrets. They LOVE having the inside secret of how to get along with the other kids. Your employees will want to know this stuff.

As a nurturing mentor (as I know you are), your staff wants to know your take on how people get things done, what influence strategies work and don't work, and most of what senior management wants and doesn't want in their reports, presentations, and meetings.

Of course, you don't have to go to each of your employees individually and do this. A simple question and answer session during your next staff meeting will work wonders.

LET THEM MENTOR YOU

Probably one of the best ways to mentor your employees is to let them "mentor" you. Hmmm... interesting, no?

Simply allow them to tell you what they know and how they see the world. Ask them how you might be more effective in their development. Observe. Listen. You'll be amazed how much you will learn.

IN REVIEW
A good mentor can:

∎ Increase your visibility.
∎ Teach you new skills.
∎ Listen to you and provide constructive criticism.
∎ Hook you up with the people you need to know to get ahead.
∎ Give you the lowdown on the politics and power in your organization or industry.

To find a mentor:

∎ Determine what you need and want from a mentor.
∎ Find one who fits those needs. (One size does not fit all!)
∎ Ask them to help you reach your goals.
∎ Take action on their advice.
∎ Get more than one mentor (that can assist you with different challenges you have.)
∎ Start a mastermind group in your hometown.
∎ Get a coach.

FOR THE BOSSES
Be a mentor to your employees by:

∎ Being a good role model.
∎ Encouraging their ideas (whether you agree with them 100% or not.)
∎ Getting to know their unique skills and help nurture them.
∎ Teaching them the political realities of the company.

I know this last chapter was like one big support group, but sometimes that's what is needed in the corporate environment.

But let's say you want some anonymity and decide to seek support outside of your workplace. Luckily, in the next chapter I reveal how to do just that!

"Write your employee ID number on all reports for Mr. Bigge. It's a number that identifies you as a person to him."

CHAPTER 7

Join The Club!

*"I refuse to join any club that would have
me as a member."*

— Groucho Marx

As I get older and a tad grayer (and yes, I do take the gray out), I have finally realized the quickest way to reach success in life. It's this:

Depending on your circumstances, it's not so much what you know that will help you reach your goals, but who you know!

Moreover, the best way to get to know influential people in your field is by joining professional associations in that field. Yes, associations are Network Heaven.

I remember about two decades ago, in my old career as an actor, attending a networking function that consisted of two sets of people: **Actors and producers.** Can you believe it?

The Hunters and the Hunted!

You could cut the desperation in the banquet room with a ginsu knife. It was a fascinating experiment in human behavior.

Picture this: Unemployed actors trying to act casual as they rubbed shoulders with industry executives who could change their lives with just a single phone call, all while these same performers did their best acting job to NOT look desperate. Sure, on the outside they're trying to remain cool and collected; inside, they're screaming to the heavens!

"FOR THE LOVE OF GOD JUST HIRE ME FOR A PART IN YOUR MOVIE, PLEASE!"

In Los Angeles, it seems, everyone wants to be somebody other than who they are right now. Having resided and worked there for a decade, I truly believe show biz folks suffer from low self-esteem and big egos.

"I may not be much... but I am all I think about!"

And here I was at a networking event where everyone was wearing the proverbial name tags that would indentify who and what they are to the other person. For instance, JOHN DOE - ACTOR would bump into a gent whose name tag might read BILL BLAH - Casting, Acme Production Company.

Being a humorist and not taking the whole event THAT seriously, I eliminated a lot of small talk by replacing my name on the sticker to read, "Can't Help You!"

Thankfully, it got a few laughs and actually opened a few doors to some interesting conversations that evening.

One was with a stunning woman who was a pediatrician, who confided in me (I kid you not) by saying,

> (sigh) "Yes, I know it's a little weird. I have a successful practice by day... But what I really want to do is direct."

Here was this stunning looking pediatrician who only wanted to be a director. I'm sure her parents were quite proud of this revelation. Four years of medical school, hundreds of thousands of dollars in tuition later, and all this creative creature wanted was to be in show business!

Of course, this might NOT have been the best networking event in the world, but show business people do what they have to do to get ahead. The competition is fierce, to say the least!

So, what about you and your success? Is networking worth it? Yes, and I whole-heartedly recommend doing it faithfully through associations that consist of "real people" working in the "real business world."

"Quid Pro Quo" or
(How to Look Like You're NOT Networking... When You Are!)

Just like any other skill you might need to learn, there truly is an art to successful networking. Here's the secret... come closer... c'mon closer... Psst! ... *the secret to getting what you want is to look like you don't want anything from the other networker.*

I call it the stealth "Quid Pro Quo" tactic.

Here's how it works. During this encounter with the other networker by the bean dip at the buffet table, all you do is the opposite of what you would normally do.

Or to paraphrase the famous motivational speaker, Zig Ziglar: **To reach your goals...
you must help other people reach theirs first!**

The Art of Handing Out a Business Card

According to Liz Lynch, the author of *Smart Networking: Attract a Following in Person and
On-line*, there is a right way and a wrong way to accept business cards. Here are some
of her do's and don'ts:

▌ **Do make notes on the back of the card.** You just met someone at a function.
Naturally, you want to remember who they are. Jot down the event and the
conversation. Anything you can do to jog your memory about the person.

▌ **Do follow up with an e-mail and remind your networking pal who you are and
where you met.** If you say something that might interest them, send them an article
or link to an article. And of course, ask them if there is anything you can help them
with.

▌ **DON'T send them a resume** unless they ask for it. You might suggest in your
e-mail that if they hear of an opening you'd be more than happy to send them your
resume.

▌ **DO look them up on Facebook and Linkedin.** After meeting your new
networking buddy, request to connect with them on these social networks. Oh,
and here's a no-brainer action to take — ignore the bland, default invitation
message that Linkedin gives you. (You'll know it the minute you see it.)

Lazy networkers use it, don't you. Instead, take advantage of this opportunity to
personalize the message by putting your personality into the e-mail.

▌ **DON'T add them to your e-mail list.** Remember, you are meeting this business
connection one-on-one. Please do NOT make the mistake of adding them to your
blog e-mail list, or any other subscriber list without their permission.

Also, the worst thing you can do is put them on a master list, then send out the
e-mail and everyone sees other e-mail addresses in the cc (copy) line. This is a no-
no. Send unsolicited e-mails and you can be accused of SPAMMING.

▌ **DO organize your business cards.** When you get the card and all the contact
info, put it into a spreadsheet or on any on-line software directory you might use.
And of course, don't forget to make a note about how you met them.

Either get rid of the card or file it for future use. Use a system that is the easiest for
you to use, which could include a box with tabs in alphabetical order, or a plastic
sleeve that easily displays the card.

4 Sure-Fire Ways to Find Your Dream Networking Organization

You may or may not know this, but **every field of endeavor has at least one association or club that supports it** (no matter how obscure the job or industry might be). Below are my three handy dandy steps to finding and benefiting from these helpful organizations.

1) HOW DO YOU FIND ONE?

These days, associations and groups related to your industry or field of interest are very easy to find. Simply point and click and do a web search for the term association and the title of your field of interest. Of course, you can do it the old fashioned way and hit your local library and ask the reference librarian to help you.

Ask to see their copy of *The Encyclopedia of Associations.* Another step is to do an online search for "associations (insert your industry)" and see what comes up.

Here's a tip: Check out the websites of the associations you're interested in for contact names, as they will be updated faster than anything in print form.

And make sure to see if they have a local chapter in your area with its own website.

2) JOIN THE CLUB

Once you've found the group or groups that can help you move forward and reboot your career, check them out on the web and see if they have a local chapter. Then, look for the membership guidelines.

For a monthly or annual fee, you'll get such perks as a newsletter or magazine, an online job board, and invites to meetings and networking mixers, all of which will help you see and be seen by those who can help you reboot.

3) VOLUNTEER

All associations have committees. And guess what they need? That's right! Volunteers! Here is a perfect opportunity to "get involved" and volunteer for a committee that interests you.

If you want to get into marketing, contact the marketing committee about helping them with their brochures and press releases. Maybe they need someone to man (or woman) the sign up table at the next meeting.

Yes, by all means, go and fill out those **"Hello: My Name Is . . ."** stickers the members wear. Doing so will enable you to meet and greet those people who most likely can help you create a brand new work life.

4) SCHMOOZE LIKE YOUR CAREER DEPENDS UPON IT (BECAUSE IT DOES)

Attend meetings, mixers, and networking sessions. This is no time to be shy. Have a few drinks and "schmooze" away, my friend. What is schmoozing? Well, it's a Yiddish word (now, a dead language). The dictionary defines schmoozing as "to talk idly or casually and in a friendly way."

Once you perfect the "art of the schmooze" you will discover that meetings and networking mixers are great places to make your presence known and learn more about what you want to do (perhaps helping you find a mentor).

Of course, this isn't a book on networking, but if it was, I'd give you the following guidelines that I have used in my past show business and now sales and marketing career:

1. **Listen.** Don't get so caught up in what you want that you blather on forever about who you are and what you're doing there. Listen to the people you meet and find common ground with them.

2. **Look for ways you can help them.** Networking with other people is all about give and take, and someone will be more inclined to help you if you help them — the old "you wash my back and I'll wash yours" way of doing business.

   Keep in mind that it doesn't have to be all business. Recommending a good mechanic, dry cleaner, or sushi restaurant can open the doors to someone helping you somewhere down the line. Give-give-give...

3. **Be patient.** Like any relationship, these things take time to nurture. You won't necessarily come away from your first meeting with an immediate referral, mentor, or even a job offer at another firm.

USE SOCIAL NETWORK THE RIGHT WAY

Ten years ago, there was no such thing as social networking. To not take advantage of this phenomenon is a crime against your future.

By all means open a Google and LinkedIn profile, as well as a professional Twitter account. (For your career, I feel Facebook is not a necessity unless you decide to create a fan page.)

Evaluate and update your LinkedIn profile on a steady basis. Show the world and your industry who are you and what you have accomplished. Give and get as many recommendations as you can.

In addition, select and contribute to as many different on-line groups that you can, without making it feel like a full time job!

In today's global marketplace, it's vital that you use the power of on-line social networking to help you reach goals. Harnessing the power of the Internet could even open doors to helping you start your own mastermind group with like-minded individuals.

Remember, don't write anything on your wall or profile that you DO NOT want your bosses or supervisors to know about. I am sure I do NOT have to tell you that when it comes to on-line activity, privacy issues are a moot point! User beware!

<u>Reinvention Guy's Take-Away Tip</u>: I know what you are thinking right now. "God, I HATE social gatherings and where I have to pretend I am interested in the other person!"

I say to you — FAKE it! Yes, I know you might not be a social butterfly at heart, but as you will learn in my "No Retreat; No Surrender" chapter, you have to do certain things, whether you like them or not, to properly reinvent yourself!

I have a friend/mentor who is not a fan of networking or schmoozing in social situations. But he KNOWS because of the notoriety in the industry, he gets more leads and offers of work when he presses the flesh with buyers of his talents.

And though schmoozing is like root canal to him, he does it with productive results. And yes, you can do the same thing if you put your mind to it!

Bear in mind: When it comes to networking,
you get out of an association what you put into it!

As you can see, I've given you the basics here, but the rest is up to you. Just think, out there somewhere in the universe is a group that can help you reboot your career. As Moses might have said to the Children of Israel, and I paraphrase, "My children... go forth and schmooze!"

IN REVIEW
Joining professional organizations is a great way to reboot your career:

▮ Find them on the web or at your local library.
▮ Join your local chapter of the national association for your industry.
▮ Volunteer for committees you are interested in.
▮ Attend the meetings, mixers and networking sessions.

▌Use social networking and update your skills and promotions.
Alright! Are we having fun yet? Hope so.

▌Did you enjoy networking at your association meetings?
▌Did you exchange business cards?
▌Did you schmooze with like-minded individuals (in a non-desperate way) and come off as a real player?

In other words, did you fake it and create a cool persona with your fellow members? (Of course, you did.) But most of all, have you had your fill of the cocktail franks that they serve at these events?

Good! Then let's move on to where you can discover how to learn new skills. Not just any skills mind you, but the ones that will propel you to new heights of success. (And won't your association friends be impressed!)

"Fingleworth, your drug tests show you to be drug free, but also to be 3 months pregnant."

www.mchumor.com

CHAPTER 8

Learn New Skills

"Skill without imagination is craftsmanship and gives us many useful objects such as wickerwork picnic baskets. Imagination without skill gives us modern art."

— Tom Stoppard (British Playwright, b.1937)

Now that you've got a good idea of what you would like to do, you have probably discovered some areas where your basic skills could use... and how can I say this politely... a little work?

That's no biggie. Don't let not knowing how to do something stop you from achieving your goals.

The good news, of course, is in our 24/7 wired world, it is possible to become an expert at almost anything if you study it long enough. There is NO doubt you will have to if you want to succeed in today's competitive marketplace.

Socrates once said (and I believe he said this while alive),

"Discipline is just deciding on what you want now... as opposed to later."

Knowing that, then your goal should be to read books on the subject, take classes, and attend seminars relating to something you need to know to get further in your career.

So what kind of skills are we talking about here? In their book, *Reinventing Your Career: Following the 5 New Paths to Career Fulfillment*, the folks at *Businessweek* highlight the following skills as biggies:

SKILL #1: YOUR HEALTH
You don't want to climb that corporate ladder all the way to the top, only to find yourself out of breath. Good health is important. Get plenty of sleep, eat right, exercise, and avoid alcohol and drugs. Naturally, you should consult your doctor before starting an exercise program.

SKILL #2: COMMUNICATION
Throughout the past 20 years, the *American Assembly of Collegiate Schools of Business* has conducted many studies on the importance of communication skills in the workplace.

And every one of them ranked written and oral communication among the top communication skills you need to succeed.

So what types of communication are we talking about here?

INTERPERSONAL
This includes all the one-on-one, face-to-face communication with other people, as well as communicating done via the phone or E-mail.

GROUP
This is crucial if you are now in, or are aiming for a position where you will be taking a lot of meetings.

PUBLIC SPEAKING
In survey after survey, public speaking has been found to be the number one fear in America.

Most people are more afraid of dying than of getting up in front of a room full of people and giving a speech or presentation. It can be nerve-racking, to be sure. And throughout my career as a stand-up comedian, and later, a speaker, I've been there... several times.

But this fear, like anything else, can be overcome with dedication and practice.

There is NO getting around it. Top-Gun business people, politicians, and entrepreneurs have moved people to action and made mountains of money when they persuaded their targeted audience to see it "their way."

Once more with gusto, this skill can be learned through effective public speaking. You can help boost your skill level by joining the *National Speaker's Association*, or local chapter. (And of course, there are my programs found at www.publicspeaklikeapro.com.)

Yes, guilty as charged. A shameless plug, but a good website with articles and programs that can help you with getting over stage fright, constructing a speech, and of course, adding humor to every presentation.

WRITING
This is a no-brainer, and no doubt, you probably know this yourself — *words motivate and move people to action*. Without a doubt, the right words tell the story of your organization and what it stands for.

Crafting the right message brands your company's message into the hearts and minds of your customers. Yes, skilled writers go far in ANY organization.

SKILL # 3: NETWORKING

Now, you might not consider networking that important where you are, thinking all that meet and greet stuff is for entrepreneurs and job-seekers. Not so. As I outlined in the earlier chapter, **networking is just getting in touch with people and forming mutually beneficial relationships.**

You'll need to know how to network to get in front of colleagues in other departments who can help you get where you want to be.

SKILL # 4: CREATIVITY

You may not think of your current job (or any job in your company or industry), as being particularly creative. But the fact is that many corporate jobs require loads of creativity.

1. **Managers** have to come up with new ideas and implement old ideas in new ways.
2. **Non-managers** (who might eventually become managers) must suggest new ideas to their superiors when asked. It doesn't get any more creative than that. This is where you definitely use right brain and left brain thinking.

SKILL # 5: THE ABILITY TO CHANGE

Let's go back to your grandparent's time where "sameness" was the name of the game. "Ahhh, the good old days." Here were the rules of the game: Just do as you were told to do… don't rock the boat… be a team player… and/or any other cliché you can come up with. (Just do that and you will be rewarded.)

And what does that mean? Well, it means, just go into work and do the same job eight (or more) hours a day for the next 40 years and you could expect regular raises and promotions. (Give the rat his cheese.)

Oh, how THAT landscaped has changed, hasn't it?

The secret to toughing it out these days in uncertain economic times is having the ability to adapt to rapid, sometimes even sudden, change. (Zig when everyone else Zags.)

So what's the secret to adapting to the "C" word (change)? You simply…

Step Out of Your Comfort Zone

That's right! Stop playing it safe! Often we take on jobs that feel secure and comfortable. The work is often challenging, but it also offers structure and stability we feel we could not do without. (All I need is my cubicle and I am a happy camper.)

But, it's more than having a steady paycheck, isn't it! It's knowing that you could be doing the same thing for eight hours a day... parking in the same spot... for the next four decades. That, surprisingly enough, is quite comforting for most people.

WARNING: You've got to take action and do things that you do not necessarily want to do, but need to be done. Situations change and your safe job might not be all that safe.

Remember those dot com companies that littered the corporate landscape of the early 1990s? Oh, sure, back then it was easy street with the money they were throwing away. Capital Vulture, I mean (clears throat), Venture Capital folks would meet earnest entrepreneurs who would then pitch them "their visions" for their company. Ventura Capital Vulture's response:

> "WOW! Great pitch! Horrible business model! It'll never work... So how many millions can we give you?!"

Yes, it was the Wild, Wild West back then. Silicon Valley workers *thought* they were safe, even though many of them worked for start-ups with no product or no service and were paid entirely in stock options. So ask yourself right now:

Will your industry be any less stable next week, next month, or even tomorrow?

Here's a scary yet enriching thought — pretend that it won't be, and figure out what you would do if something happened.

What new skills would you need? Where would you go? What would you do next? **Explore your safety zone** and then consider how wide it is.

On a piece of paper, jot down how many different skills you are comfortable using. Then decide how many different types of corporate cultures you can comfortably exist in without feeling overwhelmed and how many people you can talk to easily.

Now, evaluate how easily you can leave your comfort zone. Do you feel comfortable exploring new ideas and meeting different kinds of people? (If not, do it anyway!)

SKILL # 6: USING COMPUTERS AND TECHNOLOGY
The plain truth is everyone in the working world today needs to know his or her way around a computer. You don't necessarily need to know how to build, repair, or program them — unless it is part of your career path. BUT you certainly need to know how to use them. And it's a no brainer to learn how to use specific software programs that are applicable to your position and can make your tasks easier.

Below is a quick list of the basic computer elements you should know to advance in your career or reboot a stalled career. For those who know it, here's a review:

- **Word processing**. Years ago, a common interview question was, "Do you type?" Now it's, "What software applications do you work efficiently in?" (It's almost impossible to even make it through college without at least a basic understanding of word processors like Microsoft Word or WordPerfect. But I am sure you know this.)

- **Spreadsheets**. Spreadsheet software has come a long way, and many software packages are sophisticated enough to manage a small company's finances. Spreadsheets have a lot of bells and whistles that you might never use. Again, you should know how to create and retrieve files, add and delete cells, and use simple formulas.

- **Graphic User Interface**. Today's software is similar, whether you're using a Mac or a PC. Each program has a similar look and the same basic commands. This common look that all programs have is called the Graphic User Interface, or GUI.

Learning GUI takes time, so start by messing around with different software packages. Pretty soon you'll understand that they all work basically the same and you'll have a handle on their overall look and feel.

Once that's done, now assess your skill levels in each of these categories:

1. Are they comparable to others in your industry?
2. Are there additional pieces of software you need to learn to advance to your chosen career path? If so, how will you learn them?
3. How long will it take?

Answering these questions truthfully will let you know if you are at the right level, or need some work before you get up to your desired level. Really be honest with yourself. If not, then you could fall victim to

"The Dreaded Peter Principle"

Remember Hurricane Katrina and the ineptness of FEMA (Federal Emergency Management Agency) during it? It seems President George W. Bush, appointed his friend/crony Michael D. Brown for the position of FEMA Director. As you know, FEMA's job is to help millions of families that were stranded or displaced during this and other natural disasters.

Unfortunately, Brown was the wrong appointee ... at the wrong time. The major challenge thrown at this hapless fellow was that he couldn't properly coordinate efforts between subordinate agencies (Red Cross and state departments, etc.) and his own FEMA.

How could this have happened? Simply put, Brown had risen to a job with new responsibilities that was NOT suited for his skills and he couldn't fulfill the requirements.

Prior to this appointment, Brown served as the commissioner of judge for the *International Arabian Horse Association.* Yes, he excelled with that particular employment, but could NOT handle the new and greater responsibilities of FEMA.

In a nutshell, this man got in over his head and with the negative press coverage and the world knew it. Brown asked to be removed as the FEMA director by asking the famous question, "Can I quit now?"

Regrettably, this style of moving up the corporate food chain is a sign of the times is called "The Peter Principle." (And no, it has nothing to do with me.)

Promotions like Brown's occur a lot in business and especially in government bureaucracies. A person does really well at a particular job and is then rewarded with a promotion that exceeds his field of expertise.

"The Peter Principle" was an observation put forth in the 60s by Dr. Laurence J. Peter, a psychologist and professor of education [source: Business Open Learning Archive]. The Good Doctor put it all into perspective by saying...

> "In a hierarchically structured administration, people tend to be promoted up to their level of incompetence,"

...or, as Dr. Peter went on to explain in simpler terms, "The cream rises until it sours." So monumental is "The Peter Principle" that it has even found its way into Masters of Business Administration (MBA) curriculum.

I don't know about you, but I've seen a lot of people who have been promoted in the business and entertainment world who are card carrying members of "The Peter Principle Club."

Perhaps you've experienced it firsthand during your work life experience. It boggles the mind when you think, "How in God's name did they land this gig? Whose Uncle got her THAT job?"

I never want that to happen to you. I want you earn your stripes through dedication, perseverance and preparedness so when opportunity strikes for a promotion you are well armed to serve to the best of your abilities.

TRANSFERABLE SKILLS

Now that we've got a list of all the big, broad skills everyone needs, let's look at a few skills you might not even know you have.

These are called *transferable skills*, because they translate well from one type of job to another, whether you think so or not.

Here goes. Many of the most important career skills are not limited to use within a single type of work or occupation. Believe it or not, many skills that are valued in one area can easily be transferred to another.

You Do Have "The Right Stuff!"

Originally, I was trained as an actor, voice over specialist, and screen writer. Now, I spend the great bulk of my professional life writing sales copy for alternative health direct marketers, speaking at corporate events, and creating information products.

Wondering how my original skills helped in my new career?

Well, my background in theatre and comedy helped propel me to new heights in the speaking world. (When you've performed or spoken in front of every type of audience for over 30 years, you get in-the-trenches experience for communicating in front of sober corporate types.)

Secondly, my background as a screenwriter plus my ability to motivate audiences (with humor) allowed me to transfer those skills to the world of advertising copywriting.

Why? Because it is a sales writer's job to hit the hot buttons of his audience and to motivate them to buy a product or service.

Understanding different audiences and getting into their heads and moving them to action became second nature to me. I just took my past background and used it to my advantage.

The best part is if you believe in yourself and dig deep, you can easily do the same with your present career.

I knew a woman who left the financial world of mortgage lending (after the housing debacle) and entered into non-profit. It was a completely different universe.

She almost didn't get hired. THAT is, until she explained to her potential new bosses that she had "the right stuff" to bring to her new gig. Guess what? They clearly saw her vision and hired her for the special skills she brought to the table!

Dig deep and be honest with yourself. Do you have "the right stuff"? I bet you do, and if you don't, then now's the time to get it!

So, what are these particular in-demand skills? Well, according to Dr. Howard Figler in his book *The Complete Job-Search Handbook*, these transferable skills include:

- **Human relations skills**: interacting with supervisors, subordinates, and peers, delegating tasks, etc.
- **Research skills**: identifying people and resource materials necessary to the solution of specific problems.
- **Interviewing skills**: getting information from people when they are reluctant to give it to you or when the information is hard to get.
- **Planning skills**: being able to sense good ideas and put the gears into motion that make those ideas a reality.

By now you might be saying,

> "HOLY $*%&! But I've never actually done any of these things in a work setting, if at all. How can I get these skills?"

That's a great question, and the best part is you probably have most, if not all, of these skills already. Figler gives us three methods you can use to uncover them.

YOUR PAST
Guess what? Your skills don't have to come from your current job in order to impress. Search your past for prime examples of relevant, transferable skills.

For example, maybe you babysat when you were a kid and learned how to handle money and lead young children.

Maybe you started a pool-cleaning business in college, which taught you how to delegate tasks, market your business, interview, hire and train staff, and keep track of the money.

All of these are great, transferable skills that you can deliver to your employer when planning your "career reboot."

YOUR PERSONAL ACHIEVEMENTS

Anything (no matter how minor), can be the basis of a marketable skill set. According to Figler, **with this method you describe an experience that made you feel good about whatever it was you did.** Whatever this thing was, it should have made you feel satisfied with your behavior by your own standards, not someone else's.

I know it's tough to toot your own horn at times, but it's important for you to think about it. If it's difficult to come up with something you've done well, try thinking of something really tiny and inconsequential. Everyone has TALENT that is unique unto themselves.

ASK YOUR FRIENDS

Your family, friends, and other acquaintances can see abilities and attributes in you that you never think about. (I know, asking the family members who can hit your hot buttons is tough.)

If you can muster the courage, just ask them. You might be surprised what THEY see in you. They might bring to the surface skills you never even thought you had!

Now, make a list of all your skills. It will help when planning what you want to do to reboot your career.

SO WHERE DO I LEARN THESE SKILLS?

By this point, you've probably made a mental tally of which skills, out of those listed above, you actually have. And for the rest, well, you might be a little worried that it's too late to acquire them. Hey, I became a 2nd degree black belt at over 40 years of age!

Today's 60 is 50... today's 50 is 40 — well, you get the picture.

Allow me to give you a little motivation. If there is a skill that you need to have in order to reboot, but you don't have it, this section will show you how to get it.

Are you ready?

Good. Just know there are plenty of resources out there for learning practically any skill. Here are just a few ideas:

JOIN A GROUP

Earlier we talked about joining groups and associations as a way to network and get to know people who can help you. But you can also use the same technique for acquiring new skills.

For example, if you need to become a better speaker, there's Toastmasters (www. toastmasters.org). They have meetings in most major cities and are excellent places to practice your public speaking and get thoughtful feedback from people just like yourself.

READ BOOKS
There are thousands of books on every subject imaginable. Get yourself a library card and see what's out there. Earl Nightingale said that you can learn how to do anything by studying it just for one hour a day.

Imagine... just one hour per day, according to the famous deceased success guru, will put you at the top of your field within three years. In five, you'll be a national authority on the subject, and within seven, you can be one of the best people in the world at whatever it is you do!

TAKE COURSES
Uh-oh! More studying. (One should never stop learning, don't you agree?) You can also take classes from your local community college or other institution.

Well-known organizations like Dale Carnegie (www.dalecarnegie.com) offer several courses that can give you a leg up in your current company, and the American Management Association (www.American-Management-Association.org) offers plenty of seminars to choose from.

<u>Reinvention Guy's Take-Away Tip</u>: Toot your own horn. If you are taking a course, why not let your bosses know? They will no doubt admire your initiative and dedication. Throw in the fact that you are now working to improve yourself and it will make you more valuable to the organization while painting you as an eager up-and-comer. (And depending on the topic of the course, your company might even pay for it!)

My advice is to never, ever, believe that you're too old or you've worked in one field too long to learn something new.

That's why I wrote this book, to help you reboot your career. Yes, it takes some work, dedication, and time, BUT if you stick with it, you'll become exactly what you set out to become.

If my best friend had told me twenty-five years ago that I would be in a new line of work, not to mention be a bestselling author, I probably would've said,

"Yeah, sure... and there'll be a black president, too!"

But here we are, aren't we? Me and Barack Obama trying to change the world. (How smug of me to put myself in the same class as the leader of the free world.)

IN REVIEW

Enough pontificating, let's get back to you, shall we? Here are 6 major skill areas for you to investigate...

- Your Health
- Communication
- Networking
- Creativity
- The Ability to Change
- Computer Skills

How to find and develop these skills:

- Look to your past.
- Highlight your personal achievements.
- Ask your friends.
- Join a group.
- Read books.
- Take Courses.

Think the only way to progress in your career is to "move up the food chain?" Well, guess again. You can have a fulfilling career without doing it. No really, you can. The next chapter shows you how.

"*60 Minutes*? Thank God. I thought you were from the Securities & Exchange commission."

CHAPTER 9:

Movin' On Up (Or Sideways)

"Don't compromise yourself. It's all you've got!"

— **Janis Joplin**

If you're like most people who feel stuck in their careers, you may believe that up is the only way out. But that just isn't so. In this chapter, we'll look at some ways you can move forward instead of up.

What are your options? Well, there is:

1. **Sideways:** Moving across or horizontally within the company.
2. **Stepping Down to Get a Leg Up:** Moving down a step to open new opportunities.
3. **Temping:** Temporary moves designed for researching other options.
4. **Growing Where You Are:** Making a change without leaving your current position.
5. **Moving Out:** Just what it sounds like, this is moving to another organization entirely.

Let's take a leisurely stroll through each of these options.

SIDEWAYS
Ideally, a sideways or lateral move should mean applying your current experience to a new job at the same level, *only with different duties and challenges.* Moving sideways can help you improve your skills or shift from a slow-growing or stagnating department to an expanding part of your organization.

STEPPING DOWN TO GET A LEG UP
Sometimes, taking a step down and a cut in pay is the last thing we want. But it's sometimes necessary if we're to be in a better position for the next step on our new career path.

TEMPING
Sooner or later, we all reach a stage in our careers where we just aren't sure of what we want or what choices are available.

I like to think of this as a test-drive for your career. That's because temping lets you gather information about other jobs within your organization.

This involves taking short-term job assignments in other parts of the organization, participating on project teams with people from other departments, or even going on informational interviews with people whose job you think you want. (Of course, don't tell them that.)

GROWING WHERE YOU ARE
This is one of the easiest options and often most ignored. Basically, growing where you are means that you can expand your job, refine your expertise, and find areas of the job you really enjoy.

MOVING OUT
I know this is a book about improving your career without leaving your current employer, but let's face it, sometimes out is the only way. But make sure your ducks are in order and you've thought through all your other options first. Then when you leave the right way, you will know you did everything you could where you were.

FOR THE BOSSES
All right, bosses. Now, it's your turn at bat.

Do beads of sweat form over your lip when one of your valued employees asks you what their career options are, or why someone else got the promotion instead of them? If you do, that's acceptable.

Hopefully, you can empathize with where they are coming from. I mean, unless you bought the company, or daddy left it to you, you weren't always the boss. You didn't become the CEO or manager right out of college. *There was an ascension, right?*

I am betting that you wanted to move up within your company, so it should come as no surprise to you when an employee asks for more remuneration, or vents about another person getting a raise.

On the flipside, it's perfectly understandable to feel a little apprehensive when your best employees start wanting more. Naturally, your concern is that they will start talking to recruiters, or hitting all the Internet job sites in their off time looking for a better deal somewhere else. (And if you didn't, now you are because I brought it up.)

However, as we've seen in this chapter, your valued employees don't have to move up or out to move onward. In fact, **if you're smart and savvy (as I know you are), you can help them without hurting and losing them.**

Let's go through each of the career paths described above from the manager's perspective. Then let's see if we can come up with some concrete steps you can take to ensure your employees stay motivated and content while meeting the goals and objectives of your organization.

MOVING SIDEWAYS

With sideways or lateral moves, help your employees see that this type of move can be used to improve their skills, or shift them from a slow-growing job function to an up-and coming-part of the organization.

As you talk to employees about other possibilities, make sure they understand that you're not trying to get rid of them, but to retain their talents and abilities for the company.

Ask your employees:
- How their skills can be applied beyond their current job and department?
- What are their transferable skills?
- What other departments interest them?

HELPING YOUR EMPLOYEES GROW

As far as growth and enrichment are concerned, the big question for you and them to consider is: What can your employees do, or learn to do, that will energize their work and bring them closer to achieving not only their goals, but the goals of the organization?

With me, so far? Good! Then try asking your employees about:
- Their goals.
- What parts of their jobs they enjoy most.
- What would make their jobs more rewarding or satisfying?
- What internal or external training programs could help make their jobs better?

TEMPING

I have a pretty good idea of what you're thinking right now. Giving a talented person who is important to your team the chance to check out life in other departments isn't easy.

After all, they might not want to come back. *Ah... but there is a method to this madness.* You see, once you do, your employees will feel less trapped in their current jobs if they know they have other choices. Best of all, they may just realize that the grass isn't greener on the other side of the cubicle and come scrambling back to you.

Be proactive, ask your employees:

■ What other areas of the company interest you?
■ If you could start over in your career, what would you do differently?
■ Which departments interest you?

STEPPING DOWN TO GET A LEG UP

Naturally, the thought of a pay cut makes this option the last on anyone's list of choices. But sometimes it's the best and only way for dissatisfied employees to gain perspective, learn new skills, and try something different.

So take the initiative and ask your employees:
■ What will be your opportunities for growth in this new area?
■ Are you willing to accept a lower salary?
■ How will this new position allow you to use the skills you enjoy?

MOVING OUT

Why am I even bringing up the notion of leaving your current workplace in a book about rebooting your career in your present position?

Simply put, sometimes people just have to leave, and as a manager, all you can do is bid them adieu. Here are four telltale signs that it's time for you and your employee to part ways:

1. Their skills, interests, and values don't fit the workplace.
2. Their career goals are unrealistic for your company.
3. The employee is committed to striking out on his own as an entrepreneur.
4. Their technical skills are undervalued in the company.

Hey, it happens. Just like in romance when two partners have different ideas of where "this relationship" should go... so it is in business.

Reinvention Guy's Take-Away Tip: In evaluating our dreams and goals, we sometimes find that they just don't line up with our current company. Here's an example of what I mean. While working as an in-house copywriter for a company, another copywriter was brought in to save the marketing department.

Prior to his arrival as a knight on a white horse, he and I had worked together on some outside promotions. In fact, he was a mentor of mine, a powerful sales writer with good ideas and a very respectable track record of successful campaigns under his belt.

That's the good news. The bad news was that our boss (the president of the company) never really listened to his advice. (Which is one of his major flaws, but that is another story.)

It was frustrating to the say the least (for all of us on the team), because I knew this man had many proven strategies that could help the marketing department.

In addition, I knew if the Boss implemented them, we could have experienced huge growth at the company. Well, this other copywriter was no youngster and had some health concerns.

Not to mention there was talk of combining his company with his employer's, and thus combining resources would make them stronger in the market and lower their costs and overheads.

Well, to make a story even longer — the stress was too much for this marketer/ copywriter, and he realized that life was too short. The two had no choice but to part ways.

Here was a perfect example of an upper management employee, with good intentions, not having his vision and values lined up correctly with this particular CEO's.

No harm, no foul. Now, if you are a manager and in this situation, and you have a particular employee who fits the above mold, please do not just have the standard farewell talk with him.

Instead, it would be a good idea to go over these options:
▌ Have a face-to-face sit down with this employee.
▌ What is it about this company that's making you feel you need to look outside?
▌ If you leave here, what are your long-term career opportunities in another organization?

And really listen to him. Once you do, you may learn some things that you have the power to change. Either way, the employee will appreciate the attention and be made to think about some important issues that might have them wishing they'd stayed put, a month or two after they have left.

And guess what? You'll also increase your company's chances of keeping the employee. Best of all, you'll become known as a strategist, motivator, and people mover. Every one wins! In fact, you might even want to make up new business cards that read *Strategist – Motivator – People Mover.*

IN REVIEW
There are five possible moves in addition to moving out: Sideways, Taking a Step Down, Temping, Growing Where You Are, and Moving Out.

FOR THE BOSSES
To help your employees move around in the organization:

▌ Ask them about their goals, other departments that interest them, and what could be added to their current jobs to make them more rewarding.
▌ Know when it is time for an employee to leave, and let them go.

Bestselling author and speaker extraordinaire, Brian Tracy, says, "Your greatest resource is your time." And of course, he's right!

And in my opinion, it's a commodity that is more precious than gold... and once it's used, you may never get it back. Turn the page and discover how to use yours more wisely.

"According to the budget, we'll have to count
on body heat to keep the offices warm."

CHAPTER 10:

Time, Precious Time: Becoming a Master of Time Management

> "What I do know about physics is that to a man standing on the shore, time passes quicker than to a man on a boat
> — especially if the man on the boat is with his wife!"
>
> **—Woody Allen (Mere Anarchy)**

Here is the cold hard reality: Depending upon your situation, rebooting your career with your current employer could take some time. And to make the most of that time, you need to change how you're spending it. In this section of my book we're going to cover some proven time management tips you might not have thought of.

TIME IS YOUR MOST VALUABLE RESOURCE

Depending on how you look at it, time gets used no matter what you do with it. Of course, once it's gone you can never get it back. Compare this to money.

You can spend money on the good and the bad, but once it's gone you can always make more. Unfortunately, unless you have a time machine, you can never, ever, make more of it — only spend it more wisely than the other guy.

I am sure there are loads of people who wish there were more hours in the day so that they could do their job right.

Ah, but there's the misconception. The secret to time management does not lie in working more hours. Instead, you need to learn to use the time you already have more efficiently and effectively.

For instance, if you want to learn a new skill, you're going to have to use your time more efficiently.

My friend and colleague, Bob Bly, a successful copywriter, author, and marketer says you should adhere to the 25-50-25 rule. Say, for instance, you are learning to master a new skill. Here is a guideline you can use for your particular situation:

■ No more than 25% of your time is spent studying - e.g. reading books, going to boot camps, attending workshops, dialing into tele-seminars, listening to CDs in your car.

■ No more than 25% of your time is spent observing — watching what thriving people in your field are already doing; e.g. if you want to become a direct mail copywriter, this means reading and analyzing the direct mail you get in your mail box each day.

■ At least 50% of your time is spent actually DOING the thing you are studying and observing - e.g. if you want to sell information products on the Internet, you are creating your first product … designing your Web site … or building your list.

Now, you'll excuse me if I come off a tad Zen-like as we examine the three vital components: past, present, and future.

1. The present depends on what we did in the past, while our future depends on what we did in the past and what we are doing today. (Although it sounds like it, this is *not* an Abbott and Costello *Who's On First?* routine.)
2. The future is unknown. It cannot be controlled, BUT it can be shaped.
3. However, we have no control over the past and it cannot be modified. Again, it is only the present that we can fully control.

So, in essence, time management is the art, or more precisely, the science of planning for the future and acting on the present.

When you boil it down, your goal should be about making full use of your time potential and using it effectively.

Activities, both long term and short term, should be planned beforehand. As the old saying goes, time is money, so if you manage your time the way you do your money you can't go wrong. (Of course, if you're a spendthrift, gambler, or a shopaholic — ignore that last statement.)

I am here to tell you that you can achieve career success with less effort. But you must make better use of your available time and end any excuses. Just think: If you take care of the minutes— the hours will take care of themselves.

How Do YOU Spend Your Downtime?

TIME MANAGEMENT 101
Remember this, if you get nothing else from this chapter, or even this book: Time management is not about keeping better track of your available time, but making changes in the way you spend your time.

It astounds me that there are thousands of products on the market, from the simple to the needlessly complex, and they all claim to help you keep better track of your time. Ahh, and here's the rub, as they say... Most of them, if not all, *take away time* from your day by having to learn or implement them. The solution? You could make better use of time by simply doing what you need to be doing in the first place.

Think of it. You, me, Donald Trump, and the President of the Unites States all have the same 24 hours a day, 7 days a week, 365 days a year. It's what we do with those minutes that either guarantees our success or failure.

Here are a few tips for getting more out of yours.

DEMOLISH THE TIME BANDITS
Time bandits are the little time wasters we don't really pay that much attention to that really steal our time. Here's what I mean:

- Procrastination
- Lack of priorities
- Attempting to do too much at once
- A disorganized workspace
- Frequent interruptions
- Distractions
- Lack of self discipline

Everyone is guilty of at least one of these from time to time, with all of them sharing one trait: They all conspire to steal our time. These nefarious little interlopers of productivity make us look around at the end of the day and wonder where the time went — all while we've still got all this work piled in front of us.

So how do we identify our time bandits and cut them out of our lives? Aha! I'm glad I asked! Here's how:

START A TIME JOURNAL (YES, MORE THINGS TO WRITE! YAY!)
When some people start dieting, they first keep a food journal, or a log of everything they eat throughout the day, for a week. At the end of the week, they are often surprised to see how much junk food they have scarfed down.

What they discover at this point is what they should cut out of their diet, and what they should do differently.

As you well imagine, a time journal accomplishes the same thing. Write down everything you do each day, how long it takes you to complete each task, and what time it is when you're doing them.

This will give you an accurate record of how you really spend your time. Think you don't have enough time in your day to get what you really want in life? Your trusty time journal will show you what to cut out, like those two hours a night in front of the TV watching reruns of *Will & Grace*. Admit it, I saw you. (Wait! That was me!)

It will also help you identify your time bandits, like answering the phone every time it rings, stopping to check your stock portfolio on the Internet. Or any of the dozen or so mundane, trivial things we manage to fill our valuable time with every single day.

Now, once you've identified your time bandits, it's time to put other time management tactics into place.

SET GOALS

We've talked earlier about goal setting, so I'm not going to address that again. Just set some goals regarding how you're going to spend your time. They can be things you are going to do. Just as important, even things you aren't going to do. Like what? Like NOT answering personal phone calls or checking e-mails while at work.

PLAN AHEAD

Once your goal is firmly in place, it's time to start planning. What things do you need to do in order to make that goal happen? In what time frame? How long will it take you to accomplish this goal? Make a list of everything, and schedule the times you will work on each task.

PRIORITIZE

Let's face it, some things are more important than others (just as some people are more important to us than others). BUT for many of us, it's hard to know what those things are. That's mostly why we feel busy all day, multi-tasking. But then five o'clock rolls around and we realize we didn't get the important tasks tackled.

What do you do? You simply prioritize. That's right, make a grocery list of everything you must do to achieve your goal, in order of importance. Then, do those most important tasks first, and either hold off on or delegate the rest.

MAKE A DECISION

Sooner or later it WILL happen. You will come to a choice among two or more options for reaching your goal. Maybe the first thing you tried flopped (and now it's time for Plan B), so naturally, you try something else.

Indecision and procrastination are major time-wasters. Both are caused by fear of failure. Naturally, you want to do the right thing every time and are afraid of choosing a path that leads to losing more time or money, looking silly, or whatever.

Get over it. Make a decision and make it fast. If you were wrong, know that you can go back and fix it, even if it is a little costly. To make effective decisions:

- Weigh the pros and cons.
- List the worst thing that could possibly happen as a result of your decision.
- Decide on the various methods that will achieve your objective.
- Evaluate those methods.
- Decide on the method with the best advantages.
- Re-evaluate after the project is complete.

DELEGATE IT OR OUTSOURCE IT

I mentioned this briefly above, but this step is so important, it gets its own category. Just so you know how really special and powerful this is!

And that's because delegating and outsourcing simply means handing off certain tasks to other people who can do them better and more profitably, or just enjoy them more.

Believe it or not, this is why companies hire employees. The company founder may be very smart and a great leader, but he is probably not an accountant, a marketing guy, or knows how to turn on a computer.

What does he think to himself?

> "Let's see... hmmm... how I can grow a company and have people do what I don't want to do... or don't have time to do?" (Thinks some more, clock ticking—DING! Timer goes off.) "Oh, I know! I will get employees!"

Yes, we have a winner for best creative thought in the workplace! Then he puts his ingenious plan to work. Mr. Shrewd Business Owner goes on a shopping spree and hires accountants, marketers, and IT people... the whole shebang.

Next thing you know, he's got a whole organization of people under him who specialize in doing all the stuff that, for him, might be considered grunt work. Not that there's anything wrong with grunt work. And guess what?

There's a strong chance you are likely to be that person who will be hired by your company's founder to do the things he doesn't want to do, or know anything about!

What does this mean to you? It means you can do the same when rebooting your career, and you don't have to be the boss in order to find help.

It can be as simple as talking to your supervisor about handing off some task that you don't particularly enjoy to a colleague who does, or hiring that kid next door to mow your lawn.

Besides being a sales copywriter, internet marketer, and author, I am also a speaker. To get bookings, you have to make phone calls and do follow-up with prospects. This takes time away from my writing and internet business.

So I hired, or outsourced, this portion of my business to a woman who is a specialist and who works with other speakers – making calls on my behalf. She is a phone jockey and has a great speaking voice and is much more productive than I could be—mainly because she has it down to a science. I have also outsourced research assignments, proof reading, etc.

Look at it this way. Getting someone to do tasks you abhor (or is not your forte), is a prudent way to accomplish goals that are not a necessity for you. What it leaves you with are the tasks that are important and that get you jazzed about accomplishing.

That said, my management friends (the other folks reading this book), you actually have leeway to outsource tasks away from certain employees.

Why? Because doing so allows you to find out if one of your star performers loves doing a piece of this particular grunt work that you might hate. (Can you say win-win situation? Of course, you can.)

CREATE A SCHEDULED ROUTINE AND STICK TO IT
Make no mistake, scheduling and routine-setting is the most important part of effective time management.

Once you have set your priorities and know your long term and short term plans, it is easier to bind them in a time frame. Remember: **Once you bind them in a time frame it gets easier to achieve them and fulfill all your personal goals more quickly and easily.**

As I hope you can plainly see, it's a no brainer why you should keep to a schedule. Doing so helps you keep focused only on the tasks at hand, plus keeps you from wasting time on trivial activities or just plain goofing off. A good schedule should:

▮ Balance work with adequate relaxation time.
▮ Limits the amount of time you spend on a particular task.
▮ Keeps you from spending too much time on one activity.
▮ Takes into account your body clock and natural energy rhythms.
▮ Be flexible.

Time's A Wastin'? Here's What to Do!

A carefully made schedule is motivation for you to accomplish your work on time. It will balance work with enough self-enrichment and relaxation time. It will also limit the amount of time you spend on a particular assignment and keep you from spending too much time on a single activity.

The secret is to take deadlines and intermediary timeframes and carefully weave them into your schedule.

Again, a schedule doesn't have to be anything fancy. A calendar, date book, or PDA is sufficient. Naturally, it should be portable if you're on the go most of the time, but it should be simple. If it's too complex, you won't use it. Besides, learning how to use it will take up time better spent on knocking out your to do list, anyway.

HERE'S AN IDEA — JUST SAY NO
You can manage your time well by learning to just say "No." That's right, just say no to things that don't fit into your schedule, are not essential for achieving your main goals, or that will waste your time.

Yes, I know you want to please everyone at the Office and not be difficult, but I am giving you permission to do just that. (If anyone complains about it, just blame it on me.)

I am also aware that sometimes, it's hard to turn something down. The task might put a little extra cashola in your pocket, and sometimes it's a favor for a friend or loved one.

But before you say "yes", ask yourself,

"Self, will THIS really help me in the long run?"

Will doing this specific task help me reach one of my primary goals or advance my burgeoning career? If not, you're probably better off saying no, and your cousin will understand when you tell him you can't help him move.

Just remember, you're not denying yourself an opportunity, you're leaving yourself open for something even better to come along.

ALL IN A DAY'S WORK
Finish each day's work the same day, or rinse and repeat. Make sure you achieve this very important goal unless there is an unavoidable reason to do so.

This is the true secret of efficient time management. By finishing each day's work the same day, you are making sure that you are never overburdened with too much work.

Look at this way. If you keep piling up pending work, not only will you never really get anything done, but you'll stress yourself out and ultimately waste a lot of time.

Now, that we have some time management basics out of the way, let's check out some time tricks that will help you carve out a few extra hours per week.

UGGGH! GET UP AN HOUR EARLY

Naturally, there's that voice in your head that screams in caps,

> "But I get up early enough now! There's no way I can get up any earlier!"

I know it's tough. But after a week or so, you'll get used to it. And you know what? You'll be surprised at how getting up just an hour earlier can help accomplish more tasks that need to be done. If you haven't taken a nap by now, simply do the math and you will realize that you just gained an extra five hours a week, or an extra twenty hours a month.

Yes, we all love our sleep. Don't think you can handle it? Try it in stages. Get up fifteen minutes earlier each day, until you reach the hour goal.

So, if you usually get up at six and you want to get up at five, set your alarm for 5:45, then 5:30, and so on each day until you're getting up at five. (Your body will get used to the earlier time in a week or two.)

Imagine what you could do with an extra hour in the morning each day? Imagine finishing goals before the rest of the world and your spouse and kids get up and start taking up your time?

You could exercise, practice a skill you're trying to improve, check e-mail, or plan how you're going to approach your boss about implementing the steps you've learned in this book! It really is up to you, and the sky's pretty much the limit here.

TAKE TWO-MINUTE SHOWERS

> "What? Are you serious? That's it! Now, you've gone too far, Fogel!"

Go with me on this! Do the math. By limiting your showers to two minutes, you not only save hot water for the next person, you also save time, to the tune of 79 to 170 hours a year! Just think about what you could accomplish instead with all that time.

GET TO WORK AN HOUR EARLY

Just as getting up an hour early is crucial to mastering your time, so, too, is getting to work an hour earlier each day. Just think. It'll be quiet. There will be no coworkers, supervisors, that guy from accounting who bores you with stories about his ceramic cats, or customers to bother you. It's a great time to get a jump on your day.

STAY AN HOUR LATER

This is another surefire way to get things done (for the same reason.) After everyone else punches out, there are a lot less distractions, allowing you to catch up on e-mail, voicemail, or simply finish that memo you've been working on all day and kept getting distracted by other concerns.

Coming in early and staying late are not only techniques for getting more done, they're also great ways to kiss up, I mean — impress your boss!

Not to mention, if you're trying to move into a position for which staying late or coming in early is expected, you'll show that you're the kind of person who is willing to do it.

Here is the method to your early morning or late staying madness. Not everyone is doing it, so you will immediately stand out. Oh, one more thing... make sure your boss knows you're doing it.

ELIMINATE DISTRACTIONS
(AND YOU KNOW WHAT I'M TALKING ABOUT HERE)

This is a key step that a lot of people skip, mistaking simple distractions for important things they need in their lives. These include phones calls and voicemail, television, the Internet, and even other people.

And the biggest workplace distraction ever invented, without a doubt, has to be e-mail. But here is a sure-fire tip for dealing with it.

Answer your e-mails only once per day, preferably at the end of the day. Most of it can wait that long, but we've been conditioned to think that everything that blinks into our inbox is equally important.

Three Steps to Ruthlessly Managing a Barrage of E-mails!

Go through your inbox and look at the messages.

1. How many are truly that important and are extremely time sensitive?
2. How many are specifically addressed to you and not your entire department?
3. How many of them are simply jokes or chain letters that promise if you send it to twenty more people in the next five minutes, something good will happen to you?

C'mon, let's get real. Knowing that someone pasted a third eye on a photo of his cat is not going to help you get ahead in your career. (Oh, and I apologize to any of my friends who I sent it to!) And no matter how you kick and scream...

Seeing who wrote on your Facebook wall is NOT going to increase your time and put money in your wallet!

So, how do you battle the urge to do it? Simply wait until the end of the day to answer those types of e-mails.

In fact, you can stay late and answer a few essential ones, then delete the rest. Your supervisors will be impressed, and the IT department will congratulate you for not taking up their valuable server space with Nigerian money-laundering scams.

When we get home we're still not out of the woods. If you're like most people, especially if you're stuck in an energy-sucking, dead-end, boring career, your first inclination is probably to run home, grab a beer from the fridge, and plop down on the couch to watch reality TV shows. Don't do it!

Here's a list of all the things you should be doing instead:

- Reading an educational book (like this one) that teaches something you need to know in order to reboot your career.
- Making out your 'To Do' list for tomorrow.
- Practicing a valuable skill daily (even an hour a day).
- Setting future goals in order of importance.
- Thinking about what you have accomplished and take pleasure that you DID it!
- Exercising to give yourself the proper balance of mind and spirit.
- Reading for pleasure that has nothing to do with work.

Of course, I could go on and on, but you get the idea. Sitting around watching TV and wishing for your life to change isn't going to get you anywhere.

It's getting up and doing something that makes change happen. Robert Ringer's book says it best: Action! *Nothing Happens Until Something Moves*. In simpler terms, for something to happen in your life, YOU must make something happen (i.e. you must instigate it).

A Secret to Saving Time: Keep Your Meetings Short

Believe it or not, having a 9 am meeting to go over what you're going to talk about at the noon meeting is probably not the greatest use of everyone's time. Try this instead.

Keep your meetings to 15 minutes.

"Say what? But that's not enough time to do anything!"

Isn't it? Let's crunch some numbers once again. By shortening your meetings to 15 minutes, look at what you can cut out:

- Small talk.
- People arriving late.
- Idle chit chat.

In other words, all that extra stuff that bogs down meetings, makes them run too long, and keeps you from getting anything done.

Just imagine it. Keeping your meetings to 15 minutes forces you to go in there with a fixed agenda and a timeframe. You'll have to know exactly what you're going to cover, discuss only those items, and get out.

Of course, there is one caveat! If you're merely a team member, you won't have a lot of leeway here. BUT you can help by suggesting this idea to your boss and by simply keeping your contributions to meetings short and to the point.

My advice? If you can, take a leadership role. If others see you doing it and getting good reactions from the boss, they're more likely to follow suit and start doing the same.

KEEP YOUR MESSAGES SHORT AND SIMPLE
As the late author Henry David Thoreau said, while still alive, "Life is frittered away by details. Simplify, simplify." A great way to do this is by keeping your communications short and simple. This is the golden principle of time management, but the most difficult to follow and most flouted one.

Remember, even the most complex problem can be stated in a simple and concise manner. Do not reiterate or be superfluous while presenting facts.

For example, I know guys who do this with their e-mails. They send messages without a salutation, capital letters, or a Sincerely Yours, and they expect the same from me. They boil the e-mail down to its bare essentials.

You don't really need a "Hi Jack, this is Phil", because the 'From' line in Jack's e-mail program tells him who it is.

Don't superfluous activities (as much as you love doing them) just waste your valuable, billable hours of time?

Once you really pay attention to this, you will discover it's the little time saving tricks that can deliver a huge return over time. A good way to begin this is to make your communications short, simple, and to the point.

Here's an example. I have a friend who is quite successful, a guru in fact, within his field with many published books. As much as he tells everyone who listens to his presentations that he is naturally an introvert, when you meet him he's quite warm and approachable. But his e-mails are the opposite. They are short; some would even say curt.

One colleague commented to me about this guru's e-mail responses. I responded to him in a short and sweet e-mail,

> "Don't take offense. That's just the way he communicates on-line!"

It's obvious, this guru, a self-made millionaire by the time he was in his 30's, is a true master of his time. (In fact, he wrote a book on time management.) This marketer's goal is not to send warm, fuzzy, hug it out e-mail responses.

You ask him a question, he answers succinctly. No more, no less.

Remember: As an **intrapreneur** who is rebooting your career, your time is no less valuable. You are in charge of your destiny, so, you too, should work on getting to the point with all your in-bound and out-bound communications. Or as they say, "cut to the chase."

Three Types of Activities That Determine Your Best Use of Time!

According to Michael Masterson's *Early to Rise*, there are three types of activities that everyone does daily. These particular behavior patterns can either energize or evaporate your strength, which could ultimately stop you from reaching your goals.

Not to sound like I am from the 700 Club, but there's a good chance you might have experienced these activities at one time or another... especially if you went to college in the 60's or 70's.

Please note, I am NOT judging what anybody does, but know even the Pope might chill out at times. He is human after all. Okay, here they are (in order of appearance): Gold, Vapor, or Acid type activities.

GOLDEN CHOICES

... are intellectually challenging and emotionally engaging. I tend to put my focus on **Golden** choices because in the end, I feel I get the best ROI on my time in regards to reaching my goals. These tasks include:

▌ Watching an educational and inspiring documentary
▌ Writing a book, a screenplay
▌ Meditation
▌ Playing a musical instrument
▌ Watching a really, really good movie
▌ Appreciating art at a museum
▌ Reading an engaging book
▌ Making love
▌ Tasting a really good wine
▌ Mastering a martial art

According to ETR publisher Michael Masterson, the Golden activity/experience leaves you with a worthwhile feeling that gives you strength, along with lifting you spiritually, emotionally, and intellectually. When done, you are energized, thankful for the experience, and feel satisfied that you made the wise choice of improving yourself.

VAPOROUS CHOICES

...take place when you are in *The Mood* that leaves you with low energy and you don't want to extend yourself at that moment. Vaporous choices aren't necessarily the Devil's Work or bad. To playfully quote Jerry Seinfeld: "Not... that there's anything wrong with it."

Yes, depending on what you're doing, vaporous choice are loads of fun and don't necessarily sap your creativity. On the other hand, they also don't add up to anything more than killing time.

And yet, these actions could prove beneficial, especially when you want to gear down and take it easy, possibly at the end of the day. Vaporous activities remind me of the saying: *A body in motion stays in motion... a body at rest... well, you know the rest.*

In the end, vaporous activities remind me of doing certain guilty activities you might do on a vacation. (Think cruise ship here, folks.) **Vaporous** activities include:

▌ Going to a sporting event
▌ Listening to most mood music, including most rock 'n' roll
▌ Watching most entertaining TV, like *The Office*, *CSI*, *The Tonight Show*, etc.

▌Reading "beach" novels and page-turners
▌Having sex
▌Drinking beer or whiskey
▌Getting a massage (yes, a relaxing, soothing massage)

I am sure I don't have to tell you that **Vaporous Activities** are intellectually and emotionally easy. They feel comfortable, habit forming, and because they are, you look forward to doing them frequently.

Yes, watching mindless TV is a good deviation from the norm. In small doses it's fine, but doing too much of it leaves you with the feeling that you got mugged by the Time Bandit! However, I LOVE getting massages and I have never heard of anyone ever OD'ing on a soothing back rub.

ACIDIC CHOICES
... are, you guessed it, full of vices. And I am guessing all humans have participated in them in some degree during their lives.

Yes, even Gandhi, who I am told had a hankering for a good lap dance while sitting in the lotus position and fasting for peace. (Okay, I made that last part up.)

Step right up here folks, and allow me to tell you about our "7 Deadly Sins," otherwise known as **Acidic Activities**. Over time, these babies can destroy, reduce, or disable your body and mind.

Yes, I know a lot of celebs partake in acidic activities and *seem* to be successful (i.e. The Rolling Stones, Paris Hilton, and Charlie Sheen — every other day.)

And I am also pretty sure Keith Richards could teach a college course called "Keith Richards Best Use of Acidic Choices!"

So, why do seemingly intelligent people make these choices? Boredom? Maybe... or perhaps creative geniuses need these activities to fuel their art. (See Keith Richards.) Look, we've all been young at one time and have pushed the envelope when it comes to partying. But in the end, acidic activities (depending upon your threshold of pain) can fog your judgment and hold you back from reaching your true potential.

Please give a round of APPLAUSE to our Acidic Activities, you know them, you love them...

▌Getting drunk
▌Listening to rap music (Not all, but most of it.)

▌ Watching stupid/degrading TV shows like *Jerry Springer, Cops, The Bachelor, Keeping Up With The Kardashians...* who wants to, really?
▌ Sobering up and getting drunk again
▌ Partaking in expensive recreational drugs
▌ Waking up in the morning and being ashamed of what you did the night before!
▌ FILL in your own acidic activity

In the end, the seductive, acidic activity attracts bad company and takes you away from your family and friends.

Yes, these activities are, no doubt, alluring and intoxicating. But when it's all said and done (hopefully), you realize that continuing on this path is a self imposed obstacle, one that could easily numb you emotionally, physically, and mentally and stop you reaching success.

(Thank you for listening to this Public Service Announcement! And now back to our regularly scheduled programming.)

HOW TO GET ORGANIZED USING THE F.R.A.M.E. METHOD!

You, better than anyone, know that organizing yourself and your work desk helps reduce the time you might otherwise spend on finding that elusive memo that has ALL your vital project specs on it. To tame your unruly paper pile, separate all the papers and files using the FRAME method.

a) **F** – Finish with it.
b) **R** – Keep it for Reference.
c) **A** – Hold it in Abeyance.
d) **M** – Maintain it or file it.
e) **E** – Eradicate or throw it away.

No, Really! Minimum Stress Gives Maximum Positive Thoughts!

<u>**Reinvention Guy's Take-Away Tip:**</u> Let's face it, all work and no play makes us a tired, overworked, stressed out mess. So, take some time out for rest and relaxation. A mind loaded with too much stress cannot function in the best way, especially if the work involves creative output. (And oh boy, don't I know that.)

Relaxation enhances our capacity to work. **Minimum stress gives maximum positive thoughts.** Of course, hard work never killed anyone... unless your address is a North Korean labor camp. It is the stress associated with situations that causes health problems.

Even though I am sure you know this, it's worth repeating: It's imperative to have a healthy diet along with plenty of rest and exercise. That ends my public service message. Now it's time ...

FOR THE BOSSES

I'll make this section short, because everything I've described applies equally to those in charge. In fact, I am betting anything, you probably have more leeway to put some of these tactics and ideas into motion than your own employees, especially the 15 minute meeting tip.

How can I be so sure? Because, well, uh... how do I phrase this properly? Oh, yeah, you're the boss! And it's good to be the boss. Your house, your rules, right?

Not only that, but I imagine you've reached your level of Bossdom by doing a lot of things right in your career. Even so, I encourage you to give the above techniques a try, and ask your employees about ways their department could save time.

Just think, you might get some really good tips you would never have thought of. Your wonderful employees will feel like they're personally making a positive impact on the organization's bottom line.

IN REVIEW:

To recap, here's what we learned in this chapter to become a master of time:

- Keep a time journal as best you can.
- Shorten your e-mail communications.
- Use the F.R.A.M.E Method to banish clutter.
- Set attainable goals and the time needed to attain them.
- Plan ahead when scheduling or accomplishing certain tasks.
- Prioritize your time so it brings out the best in you and your abilities.
- Delegate it or outsource any activity that takes you away from important tasks that you HATE to do (or do not use you to your full potential).
- Create a schedule and stick to it — no matter what challenges creep into your plans along the way.
- Just say no to *time bandits* who rob you of your energy and creativity. (Yes, at times that might include loved ones.)
- Get up an hour earlier. (Go to bed earlier so you don't even miss that hour.)
- Take two-minute showers (even as much as you think I am nuts for suggesting it).
- Get to work an hour early and show those slacker colleagues of yours what you're made of.
- Stay at work an hour later and really show your slacker colleagues (and your bosses) that you are a worker on a mission, baby!

■ Eliminate or take control of distractions like television and e-mail.
■ Schedule the most optimal 15-minute meetings you can.
■ Focus on which type of activity can help you reach your immediate and long-term goals (Golden, Vaporous, Acidic).

Whew! That was exhausting. Time to take a break? No way. Don't forget: A body in motion stays in motion. In the next chapter, I want to reveal how you can enrich and Red Bull energize your contributions at work— all without changing companies.

"Let me guess,
more interoffice e-mails from Mr. Tolstoy!"

CHAPTER 11:

The Thrill is Gone:
How to Energize Your Work

"Every day I get up and look through the Forbes list of the richest people in America. If I'm not there, I go to work."

—Robert Orben (Magician, Author)

S ooner or later, it happens to all of us. We get turned off by our jobs. What once seemed exciting and new is now old and stale, and we are bored stiff, going through the motions of our jobs like *Dawn of the Dead* zombies.

What's worse is we even start thinking maybe it's time to update the special skills section of our resume and hit the road!

Yes, it's normal to think that leaving the job will invigorate us, that making a change is good... *and what we need is out there somewhere else.*

Well, I look at this way. If you are at that point, then you should approach your decision just like you were in a relationship with your significant other and contemplate to yourself:

"Am I better off with this person... or without this person?"

If my book has taught you anything so far, it's that if you put in the effort, you can find exactly what you need without leaving your current employer.

By now you want the *X factor* back in your working life, don't you? You want the magic back!

You want to get, what I like to call (and I paraphrase from Austin Powers, one of the 21st Century's great philosophers), your "mojo" back. Yes, easier said than done. BUT how does Stella get her groove back? (Yes, two movie metaphors in one sentence.)

GO WITH THE (ENERGY) FLOW
Again, it's time to do some soul searching:

 1. During what tasks are you most energetic and productive?

2. Which ones make your eyes glaze over?
3. Is there a way for you to do more of the stuff you like and less of the tasks you don't?

The key is to figure out which of your job duties give you energy and which ones take it away, and try to do more of the former and less of the latter.

First, figure out which tasks you love to do, the assignments and duties that give you energy. For example, you might enjoy:

- ▌Using your skills in new settings
- ▌Learning new skills
- ▌Having greater visibility

Pay close attention to your energy level throughout the day. Notice when it surges and when it bottoms out, and think about the difference. Try to find ways to match your desired energy level to the job duty that produces it.

Here's an idea: If you enjoy independence, look for more projects that you can do with little supervision. If it's a challenge you crave, look for opportunities to stretch yourself, such as delivering presentations to senior management, chairing a committee, or working in a new area of the company.

Now that you've identified the tasks you enjoy and those you don't, it's time to sell it to the boss. Don't panic; I'm going to walk you through it so it's easy. Here goes...

WHAT'S IN IT FOR ME (AND THEM)?
Take a little prep time and answer three questions: What's in it for you? What's in it for your department? What's in it for your boss?

The first one's easy: What's in it for you? How will this change...

- ● Increase your marketability?
- ● Improve your reputation?
- ● Help you gain more experience and self-confidence?

Think about these elements and write them down. Now onto number two: What's in it for your department? Think about how your proposed change will:

- ● Help you work better with members of your team.
- ● Increase your contribution to the department.
- ● Build new relationships and expand your personal network.

Now write these answers down. Finally, the biggie. (Drum roll, please.) **The $64,000 Question** (which, due to stagnated deflation is now about $13,000.28)... What's in it for your boss? Well, take this test and see if the changes you want will...

- Increase your value to your boss or company?
- Contribute to the company's mission or goals?
- Address a current business need?

The clock is ticking... okay, class— pencils down! Once you have thoroughly answered each of these questions, you are now ready to approach your boss.

Uh-oh... that walk to his or her office could be a long one. Dead Employee Walking? No, it won't! Have confidence, my friend, that you did your due diligence to get the results you wanted. Why?

Because common sense tells me it will be tough for your boss to say "no" to an enrichment request. Especially one that is well thought out and keeps both your goals, and the goals of the company, firmly in mind.

FOR THE BOSSES
As the boss, you might not always know that someone is dissatisfied, but they will let you know soon enough. Of course, if you're on top of things you can't help but notice absenteeism, mediocre job performance, or them handing in their two week notice.

Again, you may feel powerless to do anything about it, but here's some good news. In this chapter I'm going to show you that you're more powerful than you think.

THE DAYS OF OUR DISCONTENT
Basically, there are two employee responses to discontentment: departure and disengagement.

But either way, the results are the same: you lose that butt-in-chair human capital (you invested in), the one that was so vital to the success of your department and your company.

And as you may know already, job discontentment hurts everyone, not just the employees who are feeling it personally.

Another similarity is the message these actions are sending you. Remember: departures and disengagers are telling you that something is lacking in the work itself.

They may be paid well, work in a stable, even recession-proof industry, and are surrounded by enjoyable and friendly coworkers... but the day-to-day responsibilities of their job just doesn't provide the stimulation, possibilities for advancement, or sense of achievement that make the employee want to stay and give it their all.

A "GET ENRICHED QUICK SCHEME"

One way you can make sure your workers are satisfied and content in their jobs is through job enrichment. This means figuring out ways in which your employees can get the growth and challenges they seek without going somewhere else.

The key here is change. Job enrichment lets your employees use their creativity and independence to find new ways to get their old jobs done.

By now you're probably saying,

> "But every employee is different. What is enriching to one... is boring to another. How can I start a job enrichment program when every employee wants something different?"

What a great question. The answer is so resoundingly simple that you might smack your head in one of those, I-could've-had-a-V8 moments! Ready?

JUST ASK THEM

Bring them into your office and have a one-on-one with them, and feel free to have these questions on cheat sheets if you want:

- Do you know how your job is important to the company?
- What skills do you use on the job? What talents do you have that you aren't using?
- What parts of your job do you find challenging or rewarding?
- What would you like to be doing in the next three to five years?
- In what ways would you like your job to change?

If the employee gives you a deer-in-the-headlights stare, unable to answer these questions, then help them come up with ideas. Be truthful with them about what can and can't happen, and then move on to things you can do to help them find meaningful work.

Now, before you start shaking your head and saying, "Great, now they'll want more money!" Think for a second. There are plenty of factors well within your control at this time. You can:

- Combine or rotate tasks.
- Form teams.
- Create forms of feedback.
- Involve them in the higher functions of the organization, such as budgeting and hiring.
- Nurture their creativity.
- Set goals.
- Offer telecommuting and flextime. (Employees LOVE flextime!)

Reinvention Guy's Take-Away Tip: By the way, I am not just creating these ideas out of thin air. These are all real enrichment activities that have been put into place by corporate managers at actual companies.

Not only that, but there are probably a whole lot more that haven't even been thought of yet. Again, the possibilities are limited only by your imagination and willingness to try new things.

You don't have to go somewhere else to find more enriching, rewarding work.

And you certainly don't have to wait until your boss hands you, on a silver platter, an opportunity to learn or do something new. Here's an idea: Find a way to enrich your work, or discover a new and profitable stream no one has thought of. Present it to your boss... and just go for it.

IN REVIEW
To increase your energy at work:

- Figure out when you're most energetic and productive.
- Determine what the changes you want will do for you and your boss.
- Ask for what you want.

FOR THE BOSSES
To keep your employees more engaged and enriched on the job:

- Create a job enrichment program.
- Ask them what they want.
- Consider alternatives such as task rotation, telecommuting, and flextime.

As I hope you will agree, opportunities are all around us, especially in the workplace. The problem is you don't always perceive them. The next chapter discusses how to see what is clearly in front of you...

While at work a frustrated McWit continually bangs his head against the wall. Why? Because when he stops it feels soooooo good!

CHAPTER 12

Recognizing Opportunity!

*"Why is it whenever opportunity knocks,
I'm always in the shower?!"*

—Peter Fogel

I need to thank you for reading this far into my book. I know rebooting can be a challenge, but the rewards can be significant... just in case you just joined us and skipped to this chapter!

With the hopes of sounding like a broken record, my purpose is to have you find a new challenging and rewarding career without leaving your current employer to go someplace else.

Yes, everything you want and need could be right here at your present gig! Let's uncover opportunities at your current employer that you may not have realized were there.

Here is where you become an opportunity-seeker. (NOT a kiss-butt!) The question of course is... do you fit the fold? And by that I mean:

- Do you volunteer to take on tasks and challenges new to your position?
- Do you attend more seminars, workshops, and conferences than everyone else?
- Do you keep on top of trends affecting your profession or industry?
- Do you work on developing and increasing your skills?
- Are you actively involved in professional groups relevant to your field?
- Do you develop and maintain relationships with people at many levels throughout your organization?
- Do you turn to other people as resources to help you in your career growth?

Congratulations! If you answered 'yes' to most of these questions, you are a certified Opportunity-Seeker and you've just taken the express train (no stops) on your way to a better and brighter future. (Audience of peers: CHEER!)

Now, if you answered 'no' to more than half of these questions, well (shaking his head), you've got some work to do. Below are three steps you need to take to become a lean, mean, opportunity-seeking machine!

■ Seek opportunities that may not be obvious.
■ See opportunities that are relevant to you.
■ Seize opportunities by taking immediate action.

SEEK AND YE SHALL FIND

Just as being in love means never having to say you're sorry, seeking opportunities means always being on the lookout. Keeping your *intrapreneurial* eyes and ears open and alert for anything that might be a better opportunity for you. Once you sense it, go for it!

■ Ask your bosses or colleagues what upcoming task forces, committees, or projects are going to be a pain to staff.
■ Read your company's newsletter to see what management has planned for the future.
■ Talk to your HR department about any upcoming openings or changes that may lead to an opportunity for you.

Of course, seeing opportunities means going beyond what is right in front of you. It means thinking outside the cubicle and beyond the walls of your department to look for ways you can enrich your work and add value to your company as a whole in the process.

And don't worry if others in your department catch you in the act of being an opportunity seeker. In fact, if anyone does, smile, my friend, because there might be a "buzz" around you now.

So what is the secret to improving your ability to see opportunities? Well, it's...

■ Thinking creatively.
■ Seeing the other side of the problem.
■ Thinking beyond your usual job description.

The point is opportunities surround you every day. The challenge, of course, is to discover how to look for them, instead of waiting for your boss to hand them to you on a silver platter.

As I mentioned earlier, entrepreneurs (regardless of the shape and size they come in) will always be go-getters because they have trained their minds to see opportunities for their own business that their competition does not see.

Just like an athlete trains a certain way to win, so should entrepreneurs train themselves in a certain way.

And what is that? Two words: to succeed. They know they have a choice. It's in their psychological make-up to keep moving forward, so they can't help but notice their competition in their rear view mirror!

Let's exploit the sports analogy even more, if you don't mind...

A long distance runner is going forward, seeing the finish line in the distance. And even though he is doing that, he knows he has to take evasive action and pace himself a certain way during his race.

Common sense and experience tells the runner NOT to expend all his energy before he reaches his goal. Why? *Because he knows there are other runners at his heels.* It's the same with entrepreneurs.

Intrapreneurs who want to ascend to Star or Superstar status are self-motivated and make tactical maneuvers to outrun their competition!

On the flip side, as a worker who gets a weekly paycheck, perhaps you feel you shouldn't have to stretch or come up with new ideas for revenue for your company if your pay scale does not change.

Regrettably, that might be what is holding you back — your own interpretation of the status quo!

When I was a full-time copywriter working in the marketing department at my company, I had that entrepreneurial zeal to push us a little harder in different directions.

Doing so helped my division create different products that could compliment our present ones, thus bringing in new revenue.

We did this by sizing up the challenge and then discussing with the team how best to tackle the problems before us.

Again, I hope your goal is to create opportunities that no one else at your company sees. Accomplish this feat and you could very well be on your way to rebooting your career and spirit!

Have you found a few of those untapped opportunities at work? Great, then DO NOT edit your ideas. Instead, write them down. Investigate them fully, and know instinctively that you are on the right path to rebooting your career!

What Happens If the Ideas Don't Fly?

The answer is simply to find some more in the universe. Once again, investigate what the competition at other companies are doing.

Are they succeeding? Can you ethically "swipe" other ideas from the competition? (You don't steal, but you see how the competition is coming up with solutions in their market place.)

Get more ideas? Then seize them like a pit-bull would seize Michael Vick's head in a vise grip. Remember: Do not let go until you have exhausted ALL possibilities.

Again, for many rebooters, this is the tricky part. Everyone has tales of that business opportunity they *almost* bought into, the girl they *almost* asked to the prom, or the exciting job they *almost* took at the fun company in another city.

The secret, of course, to efficiently seizing opportunities is taking advantage of them before they slip away!

Yes, it means feeling the fear and doing it anyway. Oh, and feel free to print out the above saying and put it on your refrigerator door. Let's see how opportunity seizing is actually done with a few tips that will turn you into an All-Powerful Opportunity Seeker.

Remember: And I quote Peter Parker's Uncle Ben in the movie *Spider Man*, who said to his nephew (right before he died later on in the movie!),

   "With great power comes great responsibility..."

So use yours wisely, my Super Hero worker...

- Write out your goals, along with potential obstacles, and a timeline for completion.
- Do your due diligence about the opportunity.
- Create a network of colleagues and friends who can serve as your advisors.
- Watch out for naysayers. (They're either jealous or probably just risk averse or negative thinkers.)
- Avoid analysis paralysis. If you stall by overanalyzing too much, you could miss the boat.
- Take action! This is the most important step. You won't get anywhere in life by just thinking about your options.

Now let's examine opportunity-seeking from your boss' point of view.

FOR THE BOSSES

Of course, I'm not saying that you should become your employees' career/human resources counselor, nor am I saying that your personal mission is to guide them into a new career at work.

Not at all. What I am suggesting is you do the small things to help keep them happy right where they are, instead of them seeking to set up shop somewhere else.

We've already discussed the qualities of good opportunity seers, seekers, and seizers among employees, but the same qualities apply if you are a manager.

After all, you need to be good at finding and seizing opportunities for yourself and your employees.

<u>Reinvention Guy's Take-Away Tip</u>: An opportunity-minded manager should ask employees what types of opportunities they might be looking for and help them look — even if it means a few good people leave the department.

Here are a few steps you can take right now to seek out opportunities for you and your employees:

- Ask your people what kinds of opportunities they might be looking for.
- Ask other managers what opportunities might be opening up in their departments.
- Read newspapers and trade journals in your industry to find trends and other useful info that may affect your company or industry as a whole.
- Keep on the lookout for new projects, expansion, and retirements that might open up something good for one of your top people.

At the end of the day, there's a lot you can do to make sure your employees are seeking, finding, and taking advantage of opportunities to grow, reenergize their work, and reboot their careers. If you aren't doing your part, you will lose valuable people.

IN REVIEW

To find more opportunities:

- Ask your bosses or colleagues what upcoming task forces, committees or projects are going to be a pain to staff.
- Read your company's newsletter to see what management has planned for the future.
- Talk to your HR department about any upcoming openings or changes that may lead to an opportunity for you.
- Write out your goals, along with potential obstacles, and a timeline for completion.

▌Get lots of info about the opportunity.
▌Create a network of colleagues and friends who can serve as your advisors.
▌Lose the naysayers.
▌Avoid analysis paralysis.
▌And above everything else—take action.

FOR THE BOSSES
To find more opportunities for your employees:

▌Ask your people what kinds of opportunities they might be looking for.
▌Ask managers in other departments what opportunities might be opening up where they are.
▌Read newspapers and trade journals in your industry to find trends and other useful info that may affect your company or industry as a whole.
▌Keep searching for new projects, expansion, and retirements that might open up something good for one of your top people.

As you can plainly see, *rebooting* takes more than just time. It takes resources and immersing yourself with the right knowledge, along with an entrepreneurial zeal, to allow you to not just survive, but thrive in the workplace!

Increase your knowledge base and get your skills to a level that allows you to dominate your position. The next chapter introduces the steps to take to make that happen.

CHAPTER 13:

Keeping Yourself in the Information Loop

"Wisdom is perishable. Unlike information or knowledge,
it cannot be stored in a computer or recorded in a book.
It expires with each passing generation!"

— **Anonymous**

I love this guy Anonymous. Wouldn't it be cool if there really was a philosopher named Anonymous? Let's call him, Yousef Anonymous.

Oh, and if anyone asks, you could say he lived during the same time as Socrates, but never got any credit for any of his quotes. (Which, by the way, really riled him no end.)

Other Greeks would come up to him daily,

"Say Anonymous, did you hear what Socrates said today? The guy's a genius!"

One of the main reasons I reinvented myself was because I wanted to be in control of my destiny. To be in control of my destiny, I knew I had to soak in new specialized knowledge that would allow me to leap over my competition in the quest for clients.

It was my desire for specialized knowledge that allowed me to learn an in-demand, financially viable skill!

Hopefully, through experience, you will discover that specialized knowledge enables you to work at another level. In a nutshell, having the edge of specialized knowledge allows you:

- To feel as if we are valued for our work by our bosses and are valued members of our firm.
- To get jazzed and keep us motivated about our work.
- To make smart career choices.
- To take actions that keep our work on the bleeding edge.
- To understand the culture and politics of our workplace.

So, ask yourself right now: Are you in the loop? Do you have the latest 411 on what's going on in your workplace? If you think you do, what makes you so sure?

Here's a newsflash: Many times, we may not be getting all the information we need to feel satisfied and be successful at our jobs.

If you're learning of major changes but don't know why they're happening (or learn everything that's going on at your company from the morning news), then you need to take action on your own to make sure you are well-informed.

How do you do it without ruffling any feathers, as they say? Here's how:

YES, ONCE AGAIN—NETWORK
- Go to lunch or take breaks with other employees.
- Attend company picnics, Christmas parties, and other social functions.
- Listen for clues to the politics and culture of your firm.

DO YOUR RESEARCH
- Read your company's newsletters, press releases, and annual reports.
- Scan the Internet, professional journals in your industry, business magazines, and newspapers for industry news and trends affecting your company.
- Find out the background of any new executives. Search the company website for a bio or ask around.

ASK QUESTIONS
- Write down a few questions about the future plans for your department or company to ask your boss.
- Talk to anyone who has left the company, and find out why. (Yes, there are two sides to every story, isn't there?)
- Use Internet sites like Vault.com to access the virtual water cooler talk.

WARNING: BEWARE RUMORS
When you start doing all this asking and detective work, much of what you hear will invariably be nothing more than rumors. Oh, yes, people love rumors. They're fun to tell and more fun to believe. As you probably know, in the absence of the truth, people just naturally start making stuff up. Then these stories take on a life of their own.

Rumors may have a grain of truth to them, but be careful not to fall for everything until you've had more clarification. Take these to your boss or other trusted information source. Check out the rumor before you believe it, or worse, take action because of it.

WHY THEY AREN'T TELLING YOU

If your bosses remain mum on the subject, or plead the fifth, then you might begin to ponder...

> "Interesting... maybe 'the rumor' is true... and the entire office really is moving to South America in three days. Better load up on the SPF 90 sun block then!"

Caution: Your questions might be met by careful silence if:

▌They know you'll spread the word.
▌They're concerned about how you'll take the news.
▌They think the news will distract you from doing your best work.
▌It's not a done deal and could change at any moment.
▌They may be under orders not to tell anyone.
▌They might be too busy.

Now, if you're panicking at this point, you might be able to coax a little more information out of them.

In fact, in your quest to be *The Deep Throat* of your company or department, you just might want to give your superiors the heads up and inform them that you and a few co-workers are a tad worried about whatever is going on. So much so, that it's distracting all of you from doing your jobs.

Want an even better tactic to use? Tell them the rumor is worse than the actual information would be.

If they still remain tightlipped, ask them when they might be able to tell you something (and drift back to do your business).

In time, things will work themselves out and you might learn that what you had been dreading will either never take place, or didn't have that much of an impact on you personally, after all.

Or, of course, it might be prudent to start boning up on your Spanish for your move to South America!

FOR THE BOSSES

It's that time again, bosses, to get serious. Are you an information giver, or an information hoarder? Be honest.

Maybe it's for the reasons stated above, or maybe it's because knowing something no one else knows makes you feel all high and mighty.

Don't feel bad if the last reason is motivating you to keep secrets. We're all friends here. Just get it out in the open, deal with it, and move on.

So, how do you know what, when, and how much to share? The answer is, *it depends*.

It depends on your company's culture and upper management's opinion on the subject. If they tell you not to say anything, you can't, but that doesn't mean you can't tell your employees why you can't tell them what's going on. Just say, "I have been instructed not to discuss this matter."

STAY ON TOP OF THINGS

Believe it or not, part of your job as manager is to help your employees look to the future, whether this is part of your official job description or not.

Don't forget: To make this happen, you must keep a lookout for trends that affect your employees' development and career advancement. Using the same resources I listed for your employees earlier, find out about:

- Your organization's overall direction.
- The future of your profession, industry, and company.
- Any developing trends that may affect careers at your firm.
- The political and cultural happenings at your company.

Sharing this information with your team will enable them to better understand their roles in their industry and company, and feel confident about their future marketability. It's a win-win for everyone involved.

Plus, keeping track of what's going on in your industry can also help you get ahead and reboot your own career. Something to think about.

HOW TO SHARE INFORMATION WITH THE OTHER KIDS IN THE SANDBOX!

If you have something important to tell your employees, how do you share it? There are plenty of choices, but it all comes down to the type of news and your company's culture. Sometimes, e-mail is perfectly acceptable, while a face-to-face meeting is more appropriate for other news.

OH YES, THERE ARE TIMES WHEN YOU HAVE TO PLAY IT CLOSE TO THE VEST

Sometimes, you simply cannot share, no matter how important the info, or how tempting it would be to sing "I Know A Secret!" at the top of your lungs to anyone within earshot.

Here are some tips (and some exceptions) to keep things *under wraps* for your protection, and of course, your company's protection.

▌**Keep it to yourself.** If it's proprietary information (and you know it is), then yes, keep it to yourself, unless told otherwise.

▌**If you have information and it's public knowledge, or should be, and someone requests it** — simply give it (with joy in your heart, of course.)

▌**If you can't give them the 411**, just tell them why.

▌**If the fellow employee is NOT a happy camper with your reply,** just explain to them you are not at liberty to give this information at this time. If you must, just give them the old need to know basis spiel.

SHARE AND SHARE ALIKE

<u>Reinvention Guy's Take-Away Tip</u>: Just as sharing information with your employees is a key step in hanging on to them, you also need information from them. After all, people want to be heard. They want to give input regarding their jobs, the work, and the goals of the organization. And as a manager, it's part of your job to ask for that input.

Many managers expect their employees to come to them if there's a problem. And if they don't, it's because they don't feel comfortable — or you, the manager, don't give them the opportunity.

Hopefully you can change that by giving them the opportunity to voice their concerns, schedule weekly meetings, or casual breakfasts and lunches. And above all, perhaps you can make sure your open door policy means your door is really open and not slightly ajar!

In the end, staying in the loop, both as an employee and as a boss, is a good idea. As an employee, it'll help you make the best decisions about your career. As a boss it'll help you keep your top talent.

IN REVIEW

▌Network.

▌Do your homework.

▌Ask questions.

▌Beware of rumors (they may or may not be true.)

▌Realize there may be times when the boss can't tell you what is going on.

FOR THE BOSSES

▌Stay on top of changes in your company and industry.

▌Never, ever withhold information as a power tool.

▌If people ask if you have information, be honest and say 'yes'.

▌Tell them the reasons you are not at liberty to share.

▌Be prepared that your employees may feel you really could give them the truth if you wanted to.

▌Keep an open door policy.

What happens if everything goes smoothly at work? I mean it, it could happen, right? BUT then – there's always the chance you butt heads with a fellow employee at work who you don't, and I say this gingerly, *see eye-to-eye* with!

Going back to my show business days, I was part of a comedy writing team. When my partner and I had problems, we didn't go to human resources or an arbitrator.

No, we did the only thing two heterosexual men in their 40's could do.

We went to marriage counseling to work out our problems. That's right! The good news is YOU don't have to — if you are in the position of working with someone who is intolerable. Lucky for you the next chapter gives you some ideas to work with.

"Good news. We had 1/3 fewer
lawsuits against us this year than last."

CHAPTER 14:

How to Still Thrive While Working For a Jerk!

"That which does NOT destroy me only makes me more bitter!"
—Peter Fogel — Reinvention Expert

Your job is great. You love the organization and your teammates, the pay is good, and life is pretty sweet. Except for one thing . . . (cue up theme song from Jaws)

You work with or for a jerk!

Here's the irony of working with The Jerk! The jerk doesn't think they are a jerk. No really, they don't! That's the problem when you are *Emperor of Planet Jerkdom!*

Not surprisingly, in the jerk's world he or she is doing everything correctly, the right way, by the book, dammit! YES! They are NOT the problem—you are. Unfortunately, perception is reality — the jerk thinks you are the jerk!

There's no getting around it. Whether it's your teammates, your clients, or your boss, working with or for a jerk can really ruin your working life. And because you do, it could make you do something drastic like exit stage left from your company!

Here's an example. My dear friend, who is now a judge in California, used to work in the fraud department for a major accounting firm (that shall remain nameless). Their job: to discover internal accounting fraud with employees at companies.

SOMETIMES YOU JUST GOTTA DO WHAT YOU GOTTA DO!

My friend was a middle-aged man, an attorney who was featured on TV and in books and who had quite a respectable background working with the FBI strike force. He was by no means a pushover and not easily intimidated by anyone.

For the greater part of his working life he had his own practice and never had to answer to anyone (except judges who presided over cases of his). Well, in this new gig (before he became a judge himself), he had an immediate supervisor that he did have to answer to.

Working for a firm (and under someone for that matter) was a new step for him. To say his supervisor (an accounting bean counter) was a maniacal type A+ personality is like saying Britney Spears has a few issues to work through!

The Jerk was arguably an equal opportunity ball-buster who was nasty and demeaning to everyone. In addition, he got in my friend's face a few times more than he should have. And well, let's just say it took my friend some restraint not to land a blow or two on this man's kisser! My friend would lament to me,

> "It's getting close... I am about to clean his clock if he talks to me that way one more time."

Naturally, my friend complained to the higher-ups, but they didn't do anything about it!

Why? Because that Jerk's department was (a) making money, b) The Jerk had tenure and was efficient, and (c) The Jerk was a partner in the company.

Well, my buddy (even though he was making in excess of six figures and without any other job offers) just quit! Along with, I might add, about ten other people from the department!

These were, according to my buddy, quality people. They just couldn't take the abuse any longer!

The funny thing is that after the complete capitulation of a greater part of the department, THEN, the powers that be finally woke the-you-know-what up and realized...

> "WOW! 'The Jerk' must be really bad... a greater part of the department just quit! Hmmm... maybe NOW we should do something about it!"

Uh, hello? Coincidentally, this is exactly what they did! They bought out The Jerk (a.k.a the partner), and gave him his golden parachute (the boot, his walking papers, and any other metaphor you can think of!)

Is your present situation, like that? If so, know there is hope. YES! There are things you can do right now to take control of the situation (without quitting).

Here's How You Know If You Are Working for a Jerk!

Let's find out if you are working with or for a jerk. If you are then ONLY seek assistance if the person you are working with—

- Intimidates the staff
- Micromanages
- Acts superior
- Belittles you or others
- Makes rude, sexist, or racist comments
- Is a credit (or spotlight) hog
- Uses fear as a motivational tool
- Doesn't care
- Breaks promises

Do you work with someone who exhibits any or all of these behaviors? If so, I'm sorry to be the bearer of bad news, but you work with, or even for, a jerk.

So, what can you do about it?

You've basically got three choices. You can change their behavior, accept their behavior, or avoid the SOB.

CHANGE THE BEHAVIOR
This may seem impossible at first, but remember, you're not trying to change the person, just their unacceptable behavior.

Here's how:

- Talk to the person who is acting like a jerk. Ask them for the specific changes you want them to make, and tell them why you'd like them to make them (create a better work environment, relieve stress, etc.). Just make sure your reasons are all work-related. And let them know that you aren't judging them, just their behaviors.
- Alter your behavior to change his. Ask if he needs something different from you that he isn't getting. Put more effort into your next project instead of slacking off.

ACCEPT THEM
Try to accept them for who they are. Try these:

- Make a list of everything you like about the person. You may find that the good far outweighs the bad.
- Find out more about them. Take them out to lunch or coffee and talk about your work and personal lives.
- Thank him when he does the right thing. Hopefully, you'll reinforce the behaviors you want him to repeat — and minimize the ones you don't.

WHEN IT DOUBT... AVOID THE SCOUNDREL!

When all else fails, there's nothing like good-old-fashioned avoidance. Just stay away from this person as much as you can. Listen, if accountants can juggle books at corporations, nothing says you can't juggle your schedule so that you aren't near this person very often.

About now you might be wondering, what if this jerk is your boss?

The above techniques still apply, though they can be trickier to put into practice, and the stakes are much higher if you are unsuccessful. (Naturally, you don't want to get fired for calling someone out and bringing attention to their rude behaviors!) Just be calm and diplomatic about your approach, and you'll come out on top.

FOR THE BOSSES

Now we turn the mirror on you, the bosses. Are you a jerk?

Being a jerk includes all of the reasons listed above, plus major things like playing favorites, and not giving time off to someone whose family member has died.

Let's face it. We've all been jerks sometimes at some time in our working and personal life. Yes, we might feel that right is on our side, or that we are being unfairly attacked.

We might be bummed because of something that happened at home, or that our favorite team lost the Super Bowl, but whatever the reason, if you are exhibiting these ineffective behaviors often enough to drive your coworkers insane, then you could lose them.

<u>Reinvention Guy's Take-Away Tip</u>: Here's how to find out if you're a jerk, and how to stop your jerk-like behavior:

- Ask your employees to anonymously give you their opinions of your behavior.
- Ask friends and family members if there are any occasions where you have acted like a complete jerk.
- Once you find out, stop it. Get a coach, take a stress management course, seek counseling, and figure out what sets you off, and learn to control your emotions during these situations.
- Apologize for any inappropriate behavior.
- Get a clear picture of what your desired behavior should look like. If you know how to act, you'll be many times more likely to actually act that way.

In the end, the person most in control of how your employees perceive you is you. If you're a jerk, you'll only alienate your top people and run them off, and trust me, you don't want that.

IN REVIEW

▌To deal with a jerk at work, you have three options. You can **alter** their behavior, **accept** them for who they are, or **avoid** them entirely.

If you're the boss and your employees think you're a jerk:
▌Ask your employees their anonymous opinions of your behavior.
▌Uncover the annoying, jerk-like behavior, and stop it. Get a coach, take a stress management course, or seek counseling if you have to.
▌Apologize.
▌Get a clear picture of what your desired behavior should look like.

I hope you gained insight in how to deal with certain inappropriate behaviors in the workplace. Remember: If all else fails, you really need to look at your situation and determine if your mental or physical health is at stake when dealing with this difficult situation.

Eventually, after you've tried everything, you might have to go with the old adage: **Life is just too short**. Once you do, you'll have to make the final determination of how to deal with the angst this person(s) is putting on you and come to closure with it.

Naturally, if this step includes sticking pins in a voodoo doll that just happens to resemble 'The Jerk' — so be it!

Let's assume you've just started a new job. Does that mean your job hunt is done? For the answer, turn to the next chapter.

"Not only will it do the work of ten people,
it will scare 40% more work out of the
rest of the employees."

CHAPTER 15:

The Job Hunt Doesn't End When You Get the Job

"I like work; it fascinates me.
I can sit and look at it for hours."

—Jerome K. Jerome (English writer and humorist)

Congratulations! You've just landed your dream job. Now you can stop updating your resume, browsing online job boards, and sitting at Starbucks with your laptop, iphone, and frat cappuccino. You're done.

Right?

Well, if you want to reboot your career now or sometime down the road, the answer is no. Guess what? **Your job search doesn't end the minute you land the job you want.**

Why? Well, you can't grow complacent in your career. What if you get bored later on down the road and you haven't impressed anyone enough to give you a change?

That's why, in this chapter, we'll learn to think of our careers as an interview that never ends. Depressing thought, maybe, but it doesn't have to be. Here's what I mean.

HIT THE GROUND RUNNING FROM DAY ONE

To really get on board with your company and fit in, you'll need to know your job requirements, the corporate culture, the policies and procedures, and the unwritten rules of the place.

I know, that's a lot. And you're not going to learn it in one day, but you need to start gathering information from the moment they show you to your cubicle.

To do this, you'll use a lot of the skills we've already talked about, including a few we haven't. They are:

- **Be Proactive.** Read the company newsletter, website, annual reports, and policy manuals.
- **Ask questions.** Once you've read and done your homework, you'll know what questions to ask. Ask your boss and coworkers, or colleagues in other departments. Ask them if they are willing to show you the ropes in your organization.

■ **Connect.** Join people for lunch. Hang out with them in the break room. Volunteer for committees and task forces. Make friends. You'll not only feel like you fit in, but you'll get a lowdown on your company from the people who know it best. (C'mon, I'm not asking you to marry them.)

■ **Make yourself indispensable.** Become and stay a top performer by doing good work consistently, constantly learning new skills, and gaining a reputation for working well with others. Make sure you can be counted on when it's crunch time.

■ **Keep your resume current.** Whoa there, Big Fella! (Horse snorts.) Don't go riding into the sunset so quickly. Don't update the resume as if you're getting ready to jump ship the moment the boss looks at you wrong. Do it to keep track of your internal achievements.

The good news is that not only will it make dates and accomplishments easier to remember when you need a resume, but you'll be ready the second you hear of an opening in another department.

■ **Consider how others see you.** How do your colleagues and boss see you at work? Knowing what they now know about you, would they hire you again tomorrow? Ask a few friends and colleagues to list words that describe you. Tell them to be honest and to list any of your bad qualities.

■ **Market yourself internally.** Marketing yourself is all-important. You can be low key about it. Send e-mails to your boss every time you have a success, under the guise of keeping her informed.

In the end, you can't wait for your company to show you all the ropes and market you to other departments. **You have to do that stuff yourself.**

IN REVIEW
Your job hunt doesn't end the minute you start at a new company. Repeat after me, por favor: Career rebooting takes constant vigilance and effort.

From day one:
■ Read the company newsletter, website, annual reports, and policy manuals.
■ Ask questions.
■ Connect with your fellow employees.
■ Make yourself indispensable.
■ Keep your resume current.
■ Consider how others see you.
■ Market yourself internally.

You're a people person, right? Of course, you are. You enjoy your space, but there are times when you need your space. Well, that's exactly what I am going to show you how to do in Chapter 16!

"Remember, Art, statistics, credits and debits
are in the eye of the manipulator."

Want Some Space?

"Don't fence me in."

—Old song

Everyone needs their space. At work this means more freedom, flexibility, power, independence, and influence. How do you get yours?

Let's find out!

Experts in such matters usually distinguish between two types of space: Outer Space and Inner Space.

Controlling your Outer Space means you can select your work environment, including:

▌ Plastering your work area with family photos.
▌ Taking the laptop to your local Starbucks and working while sipping lattes.
▌ Wearing what you want (within reason).
▌ Taking the occasional sabbatical.

Inner Space refers to the mental and emotional conditions we all need in order to feel more creative and be more productive. It includes things like:

▌ Work that is self-directed instead of micro-managed.
▌ Work that is created on your terms.
▌ Managing your own time.

So, how do you get all this great space? As we've said before — when it comes to rebooting your career, all you need to do is ask.

Of course, not all requests will go smoothly. It's a chain reaction in the corporate setting. As you're aware, these days everybody seems to be answering to somebody else. When you get down to it, everybody is watching out for their own backside!

And get this: your boss or immediate supervisor might want to say yes, but be afraid to. Why? Well, she's concerned what HER boss might say. Or worse, be afraid that your coworkers might think she's being unfair to them.

The solution? Do your homework. Dig deep and think up ways your manager might say yes to your request. And always make sure you cover all the bases. By that I mean, put yourself in your boss's shoes. Think about what's in it for your boss to say yes. Well, they might include:

- A happy employee more likely to produce more and stick around for years to come.
- This change could open up new opportunities for other team members.
- The rest of the team will think the boss listens to her employees and is open-minded.
- An employee who can work independently doesn't need as much supervision, freeing the boss up to do other tasks.
- An enthusiastic, more creative employee might just think of new products, services, or procedures that could benefit not only that department, but the entire company.

Reinvention Guy's Take-Away Tip: Always think of WIFM. No, that's not an FM station. It stands for what's-in-it-for-me! Once you think what's-in-it-for your boss, team and organization, do your homework before you ask for more space.

- **Get clear about exactly what it is you want and why you want it.** How will it benefit you and increase your job satisfaction?
- **Do a good job.** If you're a top employee, your boss will want you to stay, and they'll be more likely to implement your request.
- **Figure out what your proposed change will do for your boss, team, and company.** Maybe you'll have extra hours to work since you won't be commuting every day. Better yet, you'll be more creative with your newfound independence.

And maybe you'll have increased loyalty, gratitude, commitment to the company, and job satisfaction because your boss was nice enough to listen to your request.

Hey, it could happen. Now, what happens if your boss counters with the old standby, "If I let you do it, I'll have to let everyone else do it, too"? Then try this:

- **List every downside you can think of.** Then list every downside your boss might think of and create several possible solutions for each one. So when your boss brings them up, you'll be ready to counter them with the solution.
- **Think about how your colleagues might respond.** Put yourself in their shoes and figure out how they would feel if you get what you want.
- **Collaborate with your boss to find solutions.** Naturally, your boss is worried about being fair to everyone else, so alleviate those fears. Help them find ways to give you what you want, without alienating everyone else.

IN REVIEW
There are two types of space, outer and inner. Here's how to get more of each at work.

▌ Think about what's in it for your boss, team and organization.
▌ Get clear about exactly what it is you want and why you want it.
▌ Do a great job, not just a good job.
▌ Figure out what your proposed change will do for your boss, team, and company.

What to do if your boss says, "No way. If I do that for you, I'll have to do it for everyone else." Well, have no worries. This is where the art of persuasion comes in.

▌ List every downside you can think of (and that your boss might think of), and create several possible solutions for each one.
▌ Think about how your colleagues might respond.
▌ Collaborate with your boss to find solutions.

Can you take criticism in a good, constructive way? If you're not sure, then you'll want to jump to the next chapter to see how best to give it and get it.

"No biggie... it's just the IT guys reminding you to NOT friend anyone on Facebook during work hours!"

CHAPTER 17:

The Truth Hurts . . . Or Does It?

"Having the critics praise you is like having the hangman say
you've got a pretty neck."

— **Eli Wallach**

(Actor who appeared in the Clint Eastwood movie "Hang 'Em High!")

Throughout this book, I hope you've noticed the feedback we've been getting about ourselves and how we work.

Yes, some of this feedback can be a little painful. But in reality, you need regular, honest reviews of your performance from your bosses, and even your colleagues and family members. And sometimes, the only way you'll get it is if you ask for it.

In this chapter we'll show you how. I know it can be daunting to say the least, but you'll be a better person for it, I promise.

Take a deep breath. Ready? Okay, here goes...

THINK OF TRUTH AS A GIFT
Truth is a gift. It's getting past all the barriers, niceties, and false fronts that we place around ourselves to get to what's real. If you look at it that way, then the truth becomes much easier to take and to give to others.

If you think of it like they're doing you a favor by telling you the truth about yourself, you'll be grateful for the feedback and much more eager to put their comments and suggestions into practice.

One of the reasons I gravitated towards stand-up comedy in my earlier professional life is because of the instant feedback one gets from the audience. I tell a joke or a story and I know immediately, by the response I get, if it works. No editing, no sugar coating. It's wonderful.

No matter what another performer thought of me, or said behind my back... the audience was ALWAYS the final gauge of my success.

If something didn't work; I changed it.

IT'S A JOURNEY, NOT A DESTINATION (TIRED CLICHÉ)

Yes, in the workplace, changes take time, and so does getting reviews of your performance. Here's how to get effective feedback about how you are doing with your work.

First off, you have to decide what you want feedback about. As always, you should want something that is specific about a skill or behavior.

For instance, if someone compliments me after giving a speech and says, "Wow, that was great!" I smile and thank them.

But I will then go and ask them to tell me exactly which part they did like. If they couldn't tell me, then in my eyes I didn't live up to my expectations.

I'll then ask them if there were parts of my presentation that didn't live up to their expectations. Why do I need both pieces of this information? **Because specificity is needed if we are to improve ourselves and get what we want, especially in the workplace.**

There's a reason why people move up in the workplace — get their dream position, along with a nice pay increase, right?

But enough about these other people. This is about YOU! Once you've decided on what part of your performance you need feedback on, now you have to decide who to ask for feedback. Before going to anyone, you should think long and hard about this.

Think about who can give you the best critique of your performance while being completely honest with you. Decide if that person is the one who will not make you want to crawl into the fetal position.

Again, the person who you want to get feedback from can be your boss, a coworker, your mentor, or even a close family member. No matter what the feedback is, don't take it personally... take it to heart.

Then practice your new behavior at the very next opportunity. Ask your feedback giver to critique your performance and offer additional feedback on what you did right and what you did wrong. Then simply lather, rinse, and repeat.

FIND OPPORTUNITIES TO STRETCH YOURSELF

To constantly improve your skills, move up in your company, and yes, reboot your career, you'll need helpful, reliable feedback from your boss. To get it, ask him questions like:

- ▌ If I want to move up in the company, what skills do I need to improve?
- ▌ What things should I do more of to increase my effectiveness?
- ▌ What things should I do less of in order to increase my effectiveness?

Again, take the feedback, thank them for their honesty, and figure out what steps you will take to implement the necessary changes. Remember, the other person critiqued your behavior, not you. Don't walk out of the meeting with anger and hurt feelings about something you asked for.

"That's easy for you to say. What if my boss, friend or colleague was way off base with what they said about me?"

That's a fair question, and sometimes, this can happen. When it does, you can choose to ignore it, make the suggested changes, or simply manage people's perception of you better.

If you're not really uptight, let your hair down a little and loosen up around people. Joke with your coworkers and smile occasionally. Let them see you for who you really are deep down inside.

TELL THE TRUTH (AS BEST YOU CAN)

Now it's your turn. When someone asks the same favor of you, whether it's your boss, a coworker, or a close friend, it's time to return the favor.

Your boss may really be in need of feedback. But you don't necessarily have to wait until he asks you for your opinion. When's the last time you told him that he's doing a good job, he manages his people well, or that his advice to you is really valuable?

FOR THE BOSSES

Speaking of bosses, it's that time, once again, for you guys and gals in charge to pay attention.

Do you believe in telling the truth? Of course, you do. (beat; as I wait for you to stop laughing.) No, really, stop. Seriously... we all try to, don't we? But how many times have you told those *little white lies* that get you through those sticky situations and make your day easier?

"No, honey. You don't look fat in that dress."
"You're doing a great job, Roger."

Have you ever done that?

Look, people want and need straight talk. They want to know the truth about their job performance and give you the skinny on your performance. If they don't get these things, they will suffer low morale, lose confidence in their leaders (that's you), and will stop being so loyal to the company as a whole. And sooner or later, they'll walk.

REMEMBER, THE TRUTH IS A GIFT

Think back to your school days... walking 20 miles up hill, both ways in the snow... the whole bit. In school, you probably had a coach or teacher show you something. Maybe you played baseball and were told you had to choke up more on the bat. This is just good, honest feedback, and it's exactly what your employees need from you right now, today.

Again, your job isn't to bring them down by telling them they suck. Your job is to instruct and guide them, show them how they suck, and work with them until they don't suck anymore.

The alternative, an employee who is struggling, fumbling around in the dark with no idea what they are doing wrong and thinking no one cares about their performance is what really sucks!

BE HONEST (AS MUCH AS YOU CAN!)

So how do we turn this tide of low morale and unhappy employees? Well, here's an idea. How about telling them the truth about their work? Think about:

- Their strengths and weaknesses.
- Their blind spots.
- Obstacles that may stop their career progress.

Also, please don't only give them feedback during their once-a-year performance evaluations. Those evaluations are great and an important part of keeping your people moving, but why restrict necessary feedback to the next time someone is up for a raise? Here's what you should do instead.

Every 30 days, give good, honest feedback to all your employees. They deserve it. And guess what? They'll appreciate you and the company more. Best of all, they won't feel blindsided or railroaded by problems they could have fixed six months ago had they known about them.

FEEDBACK 101

So what if you don't know how to give feedback?

Well, that's understandable. Many managers don't know how to give positive or negative comments effectively. Why? Well, perhaps they have never been taught. But more than likely, they are afraid of hurting someone's feelings, or making others feel a tad cocky when it's nothing but good news.

Here are some tips for doing it right:

- Give it in private.
- Give it adequate time. Your employee will feel unimportant if you only devote 2 minutes to your appraisal of their performance.
- Make it frequent. Once a month, with follow up critiques of their performance in between.
- Talk more about what can be done to improve, rather than what they're doing wrong.
- Be specific and give clear examples.
- Give them information that helps them make decisions.
- Give suggestions for growth and improvement.
- Let them discuss it.
- Collaborate with them on next steps for them to take.

THE TRUTH, THE WHOLE TRUTH . . .

We've already talked about this in an earlier chapter, but it bears repeating. While you're telling your workers the truth about their performance, you should also make a point of telling them the truth about what is going on the company — the good, the bad, and the ugly.

Sure, there will be times when you've been ordered not to, such as during impending mergers, acquisitions, or reorganizations. But whenever possible, you should share how well or how poorly the company is doing, and what it means for your workers.

Reinvention Guy's Take-Away Tip: Now it's your turn to get a big dose of the truth. Turn to your employees for feedback on your performance. It can be tough at first, but if you remember to think of it as a gift, and give them good examples for how to deliver the truth while evaluating their performance, you'll create an atmosphere of trust and good feeling.

And in a perfect world, this is enough to carry them through their work day with a spring in their steps and a song in their hearts. Although I've never met anyone who could do both at the same time!

And guess what? Your star players will know exactly what is required should they need a career reboot!

IN REVIEW

Getting feedback is a two-headed dragon. It feels great when it's positive. Alas, the only way to improve in all aspects of our life, and especially in business, is to get it so you can grow. Here's how to effectively give and get feedback at work:

- Think of it as a gift.
- Remember that it's a journey, not a destination. (Yes, feel free to roll your eyes, but it's true to an extent.)
- Ask specific questions to gain insights into your job performance.
- Give someone the truth when they ask you for your feedback.

FOR THE BOSSES

- No beating around the proverbial bush. Reveal the truth to your employees and tell them their strengths, weaknesses, and anything that might hold them back in their career advancement.
- Give feedback in private.
- Give feedback adequate time.
- Make it frequent.
- Talk more about what can be done to improve, rather than what they're doing wrong.
- Be specific and give clear examples.
- Give them information that helps them make decisions.
- Give suggestions for growth and improvement.
- Let them discuss it.
- Collaborate with them on next steps for them to take.
- Ask your employees for a critique of your performance.

Now for an important question that you should take to heart: Do you listen enough? Oh sure, you might hear somebody, but do you listen enough? For the longest time in my career, I only heard what I *thought* the other person said.

"Mary, please clear my schedule for today.
Something's come up."

CHAPTER 18:

Are You Listening?

"Are you really listening...
or are you just waiting for your turn to talk?

—Robert Montgomery

Here's another skill that doesn't get much air time but is very important to anyone wanting to reboot their career. It's called *listening*. Ever hear of it? It's very popular.

I'm sure you've experienced this: Someone *hears* what you said, but they didn't actually listen. But that can change. Thankfully, the good Lord gave us two ears and one mouth, so we're ahead of the game.

Common sense dictates that to get more of out of what you want in your career you need to improve your listening skills. This applies for every work scenario.

Whether it's hanging around the water cooler or break room, attending a meeting, or sitting down with the boss for some nice, truthful feedback... *listen*.

So, what might you be missing by not listening enough? Here are a few possibilities:

▎ Changes in the organization that affect you or your department.
▎ Challenges your boss is facing. Is she under or overstaffed? Pressured by senior management?
▎ How the work actually gets done at your company. The unwritten rules and informal leaders that wield power behind the scenes.

Listening is one of those skills everyone thinks they're great at. But let's be honest with ourselves for a minute. Has anyone ever accused you of not listening? It could be your boss, coworker, or spouse (especially for the men reading this)... it doesn't matter. We've all done it. And we all have legitimate (at least to us) reasons for not listening as well as we should. Maybe:

▌We are anticipating what we're going to say when they're finished talking.
▌We are reading our e-mail.
▌We are thinking about the stack of bills waiting for us when we get home.
▌We are wondering what we're having for dinner tonight.
▌And all the tons of other stuff we have on our plates and on our minds at any given moment.

But when people accuse us of not listening to them, they're not thinking of any of these things as possible reasons why you're tuning them out.

Instead, failing to listen sends the signal to the person doing the talking that you don't care enough about what they have to say. Worse, that they're not important. It's inconsiderate and rude, and you can really miss out on some important details, as we mentioned above.

So how does one become a better listener? Below are a few guidelines:

▌**Show them you're listening.** Look them in the eye and give them your full, undivided attention. Nod your head and let them know that you understand them.
▌**Don't multitask.** Close your e-mail and put any paperwork you were looking at aside. Believe it or not, life isn't a competition to see how many things you can do at the same time.
▌**Repeat what the person said back to them to make sure you understood what they said.** Like this, "Let me make sure I understand. You want me to let Greg help you with this project. Is that right?"
▌**Concentrate one hundred percent fully on what the other person is saying.** Try NOT to formulate your response while the other person is speaking. Don't wonder what you're having for dinner tonight. Don't focus on anything other than what the other person is saying. Yes, I know we've been so conditioned to doing this, so I know it's tough. But with a little practice you can accomplish it.

As I've said elsewhere in this book, good communication skills are an important step in becoming a valued, highly sought after career rebooter. That not only includes good speaking and writing skills, but good listening skills as well. Being a good listener is one of the best ways to get more of what you want and less of what you don't at work.

One of the most key listening skills a person can acquire is the ability to deal with over-used jargon or business speak.

Are You Trying to Fit In With Business Speak?

Are you using business jargon a lot during your workday to fit in? (Pause as you think about it.) C'mon, you know you do. And that's alright. We all suffer from jargonitis at one time or another.

"Hey, it's a win-win if we all think outside of the box, because we have a mission critical project that can NOT be put on the back-burner!"

Almost sounds like a bad *Saturday Night Live* sketch, doesn't it?

Well, guess what? Loads of companies and co-workers are getting tired of it. Yes, every industry has their own language. In fact, when I speak to corporations and associations I will try to get inside information, or a common enemy that is specific to the group and the group can relate to. I'll even go as far as to use some of their industry lingo.

Why? Because it shows I've done my homework (their language), and it also helps me relate better to the industry and the pain this company is going through.

Yes, at times, it's a cool thing for a specific company to create its own language. But after a while, if everyone is using the same jargon, it loses its appeal, doesn't it?

The finance industry uses jargon, such as best-in-breed (referring to investments). Some attorneys say they are underwater when they're too jammed with work, or don't want to take on another assignment.

Of course, using business speak buzz words is helpful for creating a bond within *The Tribe* of co-workers and business associates. In fact, some workers use it around the boss to show they are on top of their game!

Not sure if you are? Well, if you want some excellent examples go to what I call *Buzz Words Gone Wild*, or its real name, *The Ridiculous Business Jargon Dictionary* at www.officelife.com.

Below is just a taste of some in-the-know (that I didn't know) lingo that can come in handy at the right time and in the right place (if used properly):

Band-aid [v.]	To apply a trivial solution to a problem. "We'll band-aid the situation for now."
Bandwidth [n.]	The physical and mental limit of your working ability. "I don't have the bandwidth for another project right now." Let the techies keep this word, seriously.
Bang for the buck [n.]	The return on invested money.
Bangalored [v.]	Having been fired after your position was transferred to India. "Last month they bangalored our entire tech support department."
Bankroll [v.]	To finance. "We can't afford to bankroll another research project in this area."
Banner year [n.]	The best year in history for a given firm. Most likely, you're not having one of these.
Barnburner [n.]	An exciting situation.
Base-tending [v.]	To guard one's assets.
Bat a thousand [exp.]	A baseball term meaning a 100% success rate.
Batting average [n.]	Indicates the percentage of time that someone or something is successful. "We need to bring up our batting average in the overseas market."
Battle rhythm [n.]	A logistical plan. "We're not leaving that conference room until we establish a battle rhythm for this project." Submitted by Dan.
Bean-counter [n.]	A derogatory term for an accountant. "The bean-counters are coming in for another audit next week."

I don't know about you, but I was impressed with this other language. So what do you do? Stop using the lingo when others are using it too much? Or go cold turkey and repeat after me:

> "Lord, If I say … that bean counter tendered me… feel free to smite me that very moment!"

In the end, I think the best solution is to adhere to the old adage: less is more (more or less). Another strategy is to make a list of overused words in your industry and have a co-worker hold you accountable to NOT use such over-used cliché buzz words as optimize, synergies, deliverables, and actionables.

And every time you do use an over-used buzz word, you pay your friend $5... or you get a wedgie. Or you pay up $5 and still get a wedgie. Stick to your plan and you might just be able put a lid on "jargonitus."

FOR THE BOSSES

Just as your employees must learn to listen more effectively to you and their teammates, you must also be a better listener with them.

Effective listening helps you, the manager:

- Build loyalty and trust in your employees.
- Make your employees feel heard, understood, valued, and appreciated.
- Stay constantly in the know about conditions affecting you, your employees, and the company as a whole.
- Know when someone isn't happy, so you can fix it before it's too late and they leave.
- Keep searching for new opportunities for your star players and even yourself.

As we saw earlier in this chapter, bobbing your head up and down a hundred times when people talk to you is not good listening. Neither is doing paperwork or checking e-mail when someone is trying to tell you something.

The listening strategies we discussed above are just as applicable for managers, but what should you listen for? These are the biggies:

- **Input.** People want you to listen to their ideas and solutions. They also want to be heard and recognized.
- **Motivations.** What do your star players want from this job and from you? What gets them up out of bed every morning ready to come in and do their work? (Hint: You might have to ask them this question first in order to get your answer.)
- **Challenges.** You need to know what problems and challenges your employees face.

Basically, all your employees want is to feel that you know, trust, understand, and appreciate them. Doesn't everyone want that? Don't you want that from your boss?

Here are some ideas to become a better listener and foster these feelings of goodwill in your employees toward you:

- **Invite employees you don't know well out for lunch and ask them about their interests.** Practice your newfound listening skills on them.
- **Implement ideas your employees give you.** When they see you've put some of their ideas into practice, they will feel heard.
- **Notice them.** Go to their work spaces and ask them about family pictures or other personal mementos.
- **Open your office door.** Amazingly, just keeping your door open let's your staff know you are open to being engaged with them.

▌**Slow down.** Sometimes we are just moving too fast through our days to get to know and understand our employees. Take the time to slow down and listen to them.

▌**Make room for your staff.** By that I mean, clear off your desk and close your e-mail so you can give your employee your full, undivided attention.

▌**Notice your employee's eye color.** And no, you're not on a date, and yes, I know it sounds strange at first, but noticing their eye color will help you look the person in the eye, connect with them, and really see eye-to-eye with them.

▌**Notice and accept your employees' differences in the way they communicate.** People communicate differently. Remember the television show *Seinfeld*? In one episode, there was a woman who spoke so low and softly that no one could understand her.

In another, there was this guy that got right up in everyone's face to talk to them. These are extreme examples, but they are a good a reminder that you should listen to slow, low, close, and fast talkers the same as you do everyone else.

<u>Reinvention Guy's Take-Away Tip</u>: Do your best to become a better listener. I would hope we all want to. The upside is that employees who feel heard and understood will stay on your team and with your company. While those who don't will simply find another place to work, and your company will lose a valuable team player or two.

IN REVIEW
To become a better listener:

▌Show them you're listening.
▌Don't multitask (all the time).
▌Repeat what they just said back to them to make sure you understand what they're saying. Like this, "Let me make sure I understand. You want me to let Greg help you with this project. Is that right?"
▌Concentrate one hundred percent fully on what the other person is saying.
▌Cut back on overuse jargon and cliché lingo.

FOR THE BOSSES
Effective listening helps you as a boss:

▌Build loyalty and trust in your employees.
▌Make your employees feel heard, understood, valued, and appreciated.
▌Stay constantly in the know about conditions affecting you, your employees, and the company as a whole.
▌Know when someone isn't happy, so you can fix it before it's too late and they leave.

▌Keep on the lookout for new opportunities for your star players and even yourself.

To become a better listener to your employees:

▌Invite employees you don't know well out for lunch and ask them about their interests. Practice your newfound listening skills on them.
▌Implement ideas your employees give you. When they see you've put some of their ideas into practice, they will feel heard.
▌Notice them. Go to their work spaces and ask them about family pictures or other personal mementos.
▌Open your door.
▌Slow down. Sometimes we are just moving too fast through our days to get to know and understand our employees. Take the time to slow down and listen to them.
▌Clear off your desk and close your e-mail so you can give your employee your full, undivided attention.
▌Notice your employee's eye color. It sounds strange at first, but this will help you look the person in the eye and connect with them, help you see eye-to-eye, as it were.
▌Notice and accept your employees' differences in the way they communicate.

If you could be anything else in the world what would it be? Think about it for a moment. What gets you jazzed? If you don't have it for what you're doing, how can you ever think of successfully reinventing yourself?

What is it? Well, it is probably the one ingredient you need to really enjoy what you're doing. It's something you can't fake no matter how good an actor you are.

It is (at least I think so) the foundation you need to create the career you want. Lose it, then you must somehow create it again. Chapter 19 gives you the ammunition to do it!

"I like the way you handle responsibility, Ellsworth, so I'm going to blame some stuff on you."

CHAPTER 19:

Plug Into Your Passion

"We have too many people who live without working,
and we have altogether too many who work without living."

—Dean Charles R. Brown

Do you love your work?

Do you jump out of bed every morning looking forward to the day ahead, or hit the snooze button ten or eleven times?

Do you sit around on weekends thinking about all the fun you're going to have next week, or do you hate Mondays worse than *Garfield the Cat* does?

Since you're reading this book, you probably aren't in any hurry to get to work. But in any career reboot, it is essential that you plug into your passion for work. And now, we're going to do just that.

You see, most people expect their managers to supply meaningful, exciting work that they are passionate about. Unfortunately, what happens is the opposite.

Want the truth as to why you were hired? The reason you were hired was to do the work that the bosses either don't like to do, or can't do as well. Makes sense, doesn't it? I mean, if everyone was passionate about gardening, there would be no landscaping companies.

So let's find our passion and go for it!

GET CLEAR ON WHAT GETS YOU EXCITED
What are you passionate about? It doesn't have to be something directly work-related. It can also be a hobby. Do you:

- Like to fix things?
- Get a kick out of being a team player?
- Love crunching numbers?
- Desire to create something?
- Like teaching people things?

The list is as endless as your imagination. Also, notice the things you are passionate about during a typical workday. Are there any tasks that excite you more than others? If so, figure out a way to do more of that task and make it a bigger part of your workday.

You can also search out things that you like to do and make them a part of your job. For example, maybe you like writing or graphic design.

You could offer to create an employee newsletter. Or help edit the next edition of the employee training manual.

If you're a problem-solver, offer to fix some technical or organizational issue that everyone else is afraid to touch. You'll be doing your company a huge favor and reinvigorating yourself in the process.

Figure out what you want and just ask for it! What have you got to lose? (And don't say your job!)

TO FIND IT, YOU HAVE TO LOOK FOR IT

There's no getting around it... sometimes your job leaves you less than thrilled, but those darn perks you LOVE keep you where you are. Then why leave? Your passion could be just around the corner. All you have to do is hunt for it. Oh sure, it may not appear immediately, but if you're creative and patient, it'll come to you.

Here are a few tips to guide you to your passion:

- **Network.** Talk to your colleagues. Make friends with people in other departments. Ask them about what's happening now or coming up.
- **Tell everyone who will listen what you like to do, and what you don't.** Tell your boss and colleagues. They won't know you're interested unless you let them know.
- **Do your due** *diligence* **and read the company newsletters, website, press releases, and annual reports.** It's a good way to get wind of committees, task forces, and new projects before all the slots are filled.
- **Continue to do a great job right where you are.** You may not think what you do and what you want to do are related, but if your boss thinks you're a poor performer there, she'll think you're a poor performer anywhere.

MIX BUSINESS WITH PLEASURE

On the flipside, what if you're one of those ill-fated few whose passion isn't at all related to your profession? What if you love music and you're a lawyer? What if you love writing and you're a customer service rep?

Is there really a way to blend your outside passion with your work? Sure there is! Think about it:

■ Do you love sports? Coach or play on the company softball team.
■ Do you love to cook? Cook for your coworkers.
■ Do you love music? Start a band with like-minded (and talented) office mates.
■ Do you love to write? Start a company newsletter or offer to edit or write the manual for a new procedure.

LOVE ON THE SIDE
Who says you have to make your passion a huge part of your workday? No doubt, some people are happy enjoying their hobbies in their off hours. Maybe you enjoy playing the guitar or writing novels. No one can stop you from spending your evenings and weekends pursuing your interests.

If that's enough for you, then great. People with healthy hobbies, who get to explore their passions, come to work more energetic and invigorated, ready to do the best job they can, knowing that when they get home it's time to play.

In *If Not Now... Then When*? the folks that reinvented themselves actually went into careers that focused on what they did as children, e.g. music, art, etc. This gave them joy. You don't have to pull a 180 like them, but you can make an earnest effort to bring that playfulness to work. All you have do is...

ASK FOR IT
It can't be any simpler than that. Like most everything else in this book, to make real, lasting change, you must screw up your courage and ask for what you want. Otherwise, you may never get it. Again, the worse that can happen is the Powers-That-Be say, no!

FOR THE BOSSES
It's time to turn the mirror on you folks now. What are your employees passionate about? Do you know why they drag themselves out of bed every morning and make the commute to your company's building?

> "Uh, well... let me think about that... uh, I think that's Roger's department. Let him get back to you on that!"

I am guessing, you don't know. For some reason, people (your workers) actually need a motive to come to work every morning, besides the paycheck and the depleting health care benefits. I know, it's nuts, right? But it's true.

Sadly, for many years (and recently with this nation's employment environment), corporate bigwigs have used the old, "Just be glad you have a job!" line when someone started complaining about their work.

Although, I bet in ancient Rome, gladiators were never admonished like that. And on the flipside, they never complained.

> "Excuse me, Caligula, your highness? I know you think of me as a killing machine, but have you ever ONCE asked me what my needs are?"

Yes, times have certainly changed. It's a fact: Layoffs, rampant downsizing, and outsourcing have caused hurt feelings. The days when people worked loyally for the same company until retirement are over.

Sadly, there's no getting around it. Today's workers can become apathetic. They're not fired up about their work anymore, but instead of going somewhere else, they quit on the clock.

Researchers have estimated that workers show up at your door with only about 25 percent of their heart and head on the task at hand. How can you succeed with that?

No matter what the economy is doing, I promise you that your Star Performers always have a choice.

And hearing, "Just be glad you have a job!" for the umpteenth time is only going to make them update their resumes (which they're probably already doing if they've read this book), and start shaking the bushes for another job. And you don't want that, do you?

JUST ASK

So, how do you help your employees find work that gives them a thrill? First of all, you are going to have to get out of your comfort zone. As reluctant as you feel at that moment, you are going to have to be proactive with your worker.

As the worker's superior or boss, you're going to actually bite the bullet and ask such questions as...

"What do you enjoy best about your job?" "What do you enjoy least?" "What are you most passionate about?" "What work do you really love doing?" "What do you loathe?"

When they respond, think of ways you, as the decision maker, can work those interests into your employees' jobs.

In the best case scenario, give your worker more time to do the tasks they really want to do, reassigning a few of their other duties they hate to someone else.

No, I am serious. Find another worker who loves doing those tasks. Different strokes for different folks, right? Let's face it, when it comes to certain tasks, some call it hell... others call it home.

Imagine how well your department would run if everyone in it was doing only the work they were best at and got them fired up the most.

Isn't that a healthier alternative than half your team calling in sick or goofing off half the day and twittering because they're bored?

GIVE THE TROOPS A REASON

<u>Reinvention Guy's Take-Away Tip</u>: For better or worse, many people will gladly do work they don't like if they believe in the reason they are doing it. Again, this goes back to the notion they're impressed by the company's mission to make change, create a useful product that helps people, or raise money for a good cause.

Regrettably, it's easy to get so bogged down in what we're doing that we don't see its importance to the company as a whole.

For better or worse, we only see our part in it and don't know how important it is once it leaves our department to go somewhere else.

Other workers get jazzed over their company's overall mission. In this scenario it's NOT the work that drives them, but the results of their efforts that do.

Here we have folks that are perhaps passionate about working for a company that gives a portion of its profits to charity, or they're jazzed that it creates products that are safer for the environment.

Or lastly... they just make the best darn widgets for under $20 bucks, better than anyone around. (To this day, I still don't know what a widget is.) They want to know that the company they spend fifty weeks a year working for is doing good things in the world.

With both of these groups you, as the boss, have the power to make sure they see how important their work (and their company) is to the world at large. Help them see the big picture. You can:

- Display your company's mission statement on company letterhead, training materials, and office correspondence.
- Share news of what your company is doing in the outside world.
- Cross train with other departments so employees see how their piece of the puzzle

fits the company as a whole.
∎ Share news of the great things the organization is doing out in the world.
∎ Involve employees in fundraisers and charitable activities.

Remember, your company's mission or vision statement is more than just fancy PR to make your organization sound good to the media. It is a prime motivator for many of your employees to do their best work. Use it!

IN REVIEW

Finding your passion on the job is important for remaining satisfied with your work. To connect with your passion:

∎ Get clear on what you like to do.
∎ Find ways to mix what you like to do with your working environment.
∎ Enjoy what you love to do in your off hours.
∎ Ask the boss for what you want.

FOR THE BOSSES

Part of your job is to keep your star players happy, and one way to do that is to make sure they are able to express their hobbies, interests, and passions while at work. To do that:

∎ Ask them what challenges get them excited at work.
∎ Show them how important their job is to the company as a whole.

Notice how I also engage the bosses in this book as well as the employees. Naturally, if both of you are on the same page, it's a synergistic effort where you are both reaching your goals.

What really motivates you about getting up in the morning and going to the same job... taking the same route every day, and seeing the same people at work... ever ask yourself that?

Well, coming up next I get down to brass tacks as I ask you to make some decisions.

"But under a different
accounting convention ..."

CHAPTER 20:

It's Not Just the Money

"The best work never was and
never will be done for money."

—Unknown (And most likely broke!)

If you're like most people, you actually want more from your job than just a paycheck. Am I right?

Think about it... Do people who become school teachers, and firefighters, and police officers do it for the fat paychecks? Of course not.

So what's really motivating you in your job? Sure, the money is part of it, because we need money to live. But what are the other things about your job that keep you showing up and doing your best work? Are you getting enough of them?

If not, don't worry. In this section I'm going to show you how to get more of what you want without making a lateral move to another firm.

Rewards generally come in two flavors, intrinsic and extrinsic.

Intrinsic rewards are internal; they are rewards we give ourselves. Like the shiny, happy feeling we get when we do something that makes a difference in somebody's world, or teach someone something important. No amount of money can replace an intrinsic reward.

Extrinsic rewards are external rewards that someone else gives us, usually someone in power like our boss. These rewards include physical things like a promotion, a raise, a reserved parking space, or a gift card to a favorite restaurant, as well as intangible things like the boss telling you that you did a great job.

HOW TO GET REWARDED

So how do we go about getting these things? I'm so glad you asked. Just:

▌**Meet and exceed your work objectives.** Do MORE than what the other guy in the next cubicle does. Go beyond the call of duty.

▌**Talk to your boss about the rewards you would like.** (Yes, spell out exactly what you want. If he doesn't know, how can he give them to you?)
▌**Thank them for their thank you.** Strangely, people will do more of what they are rewarded for, so make sure you tell them you appreciate their recognition of you and the way they presented it.
▌**Drop a few hints like you would before Christmas or your birthday.** "I sure would like that parking space right up front."
▌**Reward yourself.** You don't have to wait for someone else to recognize your hard work. When you've reached some goal you've set for yourself, give yourself a reward. It can be a night on the town with your special someone, or a bowl of chocolate ice cream... just so long as you give yourself the time to enjoy your success, no matter how minor.

The important thing to keep in mind here is that if you're not feeling rewarded at work, figure out why, decide what you want, and then ask for it!

FOR THE BOSSES
The ball's in your court now, bosses. *Are you rewarding your employees for their hard work?*

You might say, "Hey, I'm giving them raises at certain intervals. Isn't that enough?"

Well, it might be for some. But if this chapter has taught you anything, it's that people go to work for more than the money. They spend 50 weeks a year driving in rush hour traffic to reach your company's headquarters. Trust me on this... At the end of the day, they want more than just a steady paycheck out of the deal.

They also want perks such as :

▌Challenging work
▌Growth opportunities
▌Flexible schedules
▌Meaningful work
▌A good boss (that's you!)
▌Recognition for a job well done

Many managers incorrectly assume that everyone wants, likes, or needs the same types of recognition. I am sure you know the old saying, *different strokes for different folks*, right?

What will thrill one person could potentially embarrass another. What do you do? Simple, ask. Yeah, I know, a no-brainer, right? Ask your employees what kind of recognition or reward they appreciate the most.

Case in point. An ex-girlfriend of mine works for an insurance company (at lower pay than what she got at her previous place of employment). Let's call her Carol, because, well, that's her name.

Working in this industry, at this job, is NOT a career to her. *It's a j-o-b*. According to her, it's better than being on unemployment. Each month any employee who is never late for work gets $5. And then that amount with another $5 from Human Resources. Yep, a whopping $10.

PRAISE
Of course, while every employee is different, good old fashioned praise and a nice pat on the head once in a millennium works for everyone.

Just as long as it's delivered with sincerity. Listen, you really can't go wrong or overboard here. Everyone wants to hear how valuable they are to the team and how important their work and contribution is to the success of the organization. And they never get tired of hearing it.

Are you dishing it out often enough? To praise your employees:

- When your employees do something right, thank them right then and there.
- Praise your people for specific actions.
- Take them to lunch or dinner in a nice restaurant to thank them for a job well done.
- Go to your employee's office or cubicle and thank them personally.
- Praise them in front of others, like their work colleagues and your boss.
- Send them a letter or e-mail. Copy the e-mail to other team members or upper management.

PUT YOURSELF IN THEIR PLACE
If you're having trouble coming up with ways to recognize your employees for their hard work and dedication, just think about how you would like to be praised and rewarded.

Keep an open mind here and look at a few ideas to get the ball rolling:

- **Time.** The morning or afternoon off, a Friday off, or just a free day to use whenever and however they choose can be a great reward.
- **Toys.** Theater tickets, a dart board in the break room (your picture on it is optional), or even higher ticket items can keep employees around.
- **Trophies.** A plaque or trophy can be a great motivator. Something with their likeness will be even cooler.

- **Opportunities.** Being part of a steering committee, taking a class, or the chance to deliver an important presentation to upper management.
- **Fun.** Company outings, pizza parties, etc.
- **Freedom.** Working from home, casual dress Fridays, less supervision, managing a budget.

Reinvention Guys' Take-Away Tip: Whether the bosses want to admit it or not, studies show that money alone will not keep your employees happy. As a boss, you also need to work at providing other motivational perks to get your good people to stay for the long haul.

Yes, believe it or not, your staff (the hardworking folks that do the tasks you do NOT want to do), want more out of work than a paycheck. Without coddling them, I would hope you, as their boss, would want to make sure they're getting those things on a regular basis.

IN REVIEW
There are two types of rewards: **intrinsic** and **extrinsic**. Intrinsic rewards are internal rewards that we give ourselves, while extrinsic rewards are external and given to us by others.

How to get rewarded:

- Meet and exceed your work objectives.
- Talk to your boss about the rewards you would like.
- Thank them for their thanking you.
- Drop them hints from time to time.
- Reward yourself.

FOR THE BOSSES
How to praise your employees:

- When your employees do something right, thank them right then and there.
- Praise your people for specific actions.
- Take them to lunch or dinner in a nice restaurant to thank them for a job well done.
- Go to your employee's office or cubicle and thank them personally.
- Praise them in front of others, like their work colleagues and your boss.
- Send them a letter or e-mail. Copy the e-mail to other team members or upper management.

Yes, we all like praise — it's in our DNA. But placating an employee and not dealing with their other needs will, after a while, fall on deaf ears. Chapter 21 reveals what is still vital to your career happiness. And no amount of praise will change it!

"We consult those with whom we agree,
which is why I rarely consult my conscience."

OK, It Is About the Money

"All I ask is the chance to prove that money can't make me happy"

—Spike Milligan

(musician, poet, playwright and actor)

This chapter is for those of you who just read the previous chapter and said,

> "Hey, I don't care what the study or research said, YOU did. But pal, I want more money!"

It is for those of you who are perfectly satisfied with your job duties, hours, corporate culture, bosses, and fellow employees (thank you very much), but just aren't making the kind of bread you feel you should.

Quite a few of you might be thinking that the only way you can reboot your career (or just stay one step ahead of the bill collectors), is by working lots of overtime at every opportunity.

But that's not what I'm going to suggest you do in this book. You see, it's not about working harder . . .

It's About Working Smarter!

What do I mean by that? Well, a lot of business gurus will tell you that you only get paid what you're worth. But I don't believe that's true for every profession.

You can be the best gardener, the best factory worker, the best janitor in the world, and you'll only make the going rate for gardeners, factory workers, and janitors in your geographic area.

This is because some employers don't pay you what you're worth . . . they pay what little they can get away with and still make a profit. (Not YOUR employer, of course, I am talking about other employers who aren't reading this book!)

Of course, the method to this madness is for you to find a NEW position within your own company that will pay you more. And why, pray tell, would your boss pay someone like you more money?

Simply because it's good business sense. Bosses, repeat this mantra after me please: pay more for positions/jobs that make the company money or otherwise impact the bottom line in some meaningful way. (At least, SMART bosses do!)

YOUR JOB IS TO FIND THE PROFIT CENTERS

According to bestselling author and business guru, Michael Masterson, if you want to make more money at your current employer, you must find ways to make more money for your current employer. This means *finding your organization's profit centers.*

A *profit center?* Yes, that's just business lingo for those specific areas of a business whose sole purpose is to make that business money. As an intrapreneur (again, this is someone who is in business for themselves while working for a company), you need to find the Profit Center at your firm.

FOLLOW THE MONEY

Where is the money made in your firm, and who makes it? With most companies, it's usually in the areas of sales, marketing, product creation, and profit management.

The people in these positions (CFOs, copywriters, marketing consultants, and project managers), are the most responsible for bringing in the coin to the company.

Michael Masterson, Editor and Publisher of **ETR**, discovered through thirty years of owning companies, how vital idea generators are to entrepreneurial business success:

1. In every company, there is an *invisible culture that separates the idea generators from everyone else.*
2. When it comes to ideas, Pareto's Law rules. The idea generators represent fewer than 20% of a company's employees and yet they generate more than 80% of the ideas.
3. The idea generators make much more money than the average employee. His guess is two and 10 times the average salary.

What can you take away from this? Learn how to become an Idea Generator for your boss. You will enjoy more power and make loads of more money, LOTS of it!

DO YOUR DUE DILIGENCE

Your task is to identify the specific jobs that bring in the money and the people who do them. Then you should narrow down your list to two or three jobs you would most like to do.

Simple enough, right? Don't worry about whether or not you can actually do them right now. With a little study and hard work, you can master most anything. And yes, there are tons of resources out there that can teach you any skill you could want to learn.

So, beginning right now, today, my fellow entrepreneur, learn something about it by researching it. Simply go to your local library, then look up the job in their most recent copy of the *Occupational Outreach Handbook*. Once you do, find out what it pays, job duties, and whether or not the field is moving up or getting phased out.

Look at it as if you're buying an automobile. Here you are kickin' the tires and looking under the hood to see if taking on a new skill for a new profit center is worth your time, energy, and resources.

▮ Ask your colleagues in those jobs what the daily routine is like and about any problems or challenges related to the job.
▮ Read everything you can about the job from books, articles, and blogs.
▮ Read both the theory of its practice and how to get a job doing it.

REACH OUT
Once you feel you're ready, go to your boss and tell her your plans. Now is NOT the time to *vent about how you're tired of her crap and you need a change*. No, no... in a calm, methodical way, inform your supervisor of how you've just found ways to make yourself more valuable to the company.

Then drop the sentence, "I have discovered another Profit Center for the firm!" (Then watch as they arch an eye-brow at how you just dropped that cool term.)

Once you've made your important announcement, head on down to the department of where you'd like to work, and tell the person in charge that their field is something you honestly think you'd be good at.

Don't share you're feeling with just anybody in the department. They might not know you and there's a chance you might be stepping on some toes, so go to the head of the class, the department head.

Reveal that you've been learning about their particular field in your free time, and you'd like to volunteer to help them when they need it, so you can learn even more.

The bosses will love this! They'll be impressed by your willingness to give them a hand, as well as the fact that you've spent your free time learning about their department. If you do this right, you'll also quickly get the reputation of being an up-and-comer in your company.

JUST MAKE YOURSELF MORE VALUABLE

"But Reinvention Guy, what if we work in a non-profit or not-for-profit? There's no sales or marketing department here."

<u>Reinvention Guy's Take-Away Tip</u>: It's time, again, to release your inner entrepreneur, if you want to jump to the head of the class and make more moolah!

Focus like a laser in making yourself more indispensible and more valuable to the powers-that-be!

You accomplish that feat by making yourself more valuable, which means giving your employer more value than you are currently getting in salary.

Go the extra mile... come in early and stay late... offer to help your colleagues with their deadlines, assignments, etc. I know, you're killing yourself now at possibly a lower pay. But dig deep within yourself to do what your fellow co-worker(s) won't do — and down the road you will reap the benefits.

Your goal should be to focus your efforts. Like a sleuth, match your expertise to problems that arise in your office that need fixing. And yes, volunteer and ask your boss for more work when you've completed yours.

Here's an exercise for you, courtesy of business guru, Brian Tracy. Imagine, just for a moment, that it is possible for you to make ten times your current annual wage.

The common reaction people have to this is to think about it briefly for a couple of seconds, and then start listing all the reasons it'll never happen.

But trust me, it is entirely possible for everyone reading this book to make significantly more than they are now. And they don't have to leave their current employer or strike out on their own to do it.

Mr. Tracy has a two step process for making this lofty income goal come true.

1. IDENTIFY THE HIGHEST PAID PEOPLE IN YOUR FIELD, AND DO WHAT THEY DO.
Who are they? What are they doing differently from others who aren't doing as well? Study them. Read about them. Maybe they've written a book on what's made them so successful, or maybe you can even get them to mentor you. Success leaves clues. Follow them.

2. SET A GOAL TO DOUBLE YOUR INCOME OVER THE NEXT TWO OR THREE YEARS, AND FIGURE OUT WHAT YOU HAVE TO DO TO MAKE IT HAPPEN.

Remember the chapter on setting goals? Go back and reread it if you have to, then set some goals. Make a list of what you need to know and do, and set a timeline for each step's completion. A goal is just a dream with a deadline, so get to it.

I would like to add a number 3 to this list:

3. DO ONE THING EACH AND EVERY DAY TO MAKE YOUR WEALTH GOAL A REALITY.

Everyone gets bogged down in the details of day-to-day life. Things come up, you don't have time to do everything else plus put out the fires, and before you know it, six months to a year has gone by without you being one step closer to a high six figure income.

Don't let your dreams die. Planning is one thing, and it's great, but greater still is action. Take action today and every day on just one thing on your list. You'll thank me later. (Preferably with a steak dinner.)

IN REVIEW

■ Find the profit centers in your company.
■ Do research to learn all you can about them.
■ Let managers in those areas know you are interested in those fields.
■ Make yourself more valuable to your current boss.
■ Find the highest paid people in your field and do what they do.
■ Set a goal to double your income and figure out what to do to make it happen.
■ Do one thing every day to achieve your wealth goal.

Are you a social person, or do you find yourself hiding and not participating within the culture of your firm's business? Are you a people person, as they say? If not, that's alright.

And if so, well there's a skill you should learn to use effectively if you want to leap to the next level of career reinvention.

Believe it or not, people with lesser talents have used this one skill to propel their careers to new heights. Entrepreneurs and marketers use it to leverage their time, money, and resources more effectively.

To use it wisely you will have to get out of your comfort zone. But once you do, it will pay dividends back to you for years to come.

"Mary, I've got meetings all day so I'm going to be unable to have my scheduled happiness moment at 3:01. You have it for me, OK?"

CHAPTER 22:

Harness the Power of Networking

"It isn't what you know, but who you know."

— **Unknown**
(Anonymous' First Cousin!)

Here's the nitty-gritty: No one... I mean NO ONE, reached success without direct help or leveraging the help of others. And your career reboot is no different.

Whether you want to admit it or not, at some time you're going to have to connect, link up, and network with people. Luckily, in this chapter we're going to examine how to make the best use of your time doing it.

CONNECT WITH THE RIGHT PEOPLE

Experience has shown that a job that is conducted in complete isolation is rare. (Except maybe a night watchman and his inner demons that talk to him while on patrol.)

But for the most part, you're hopefully working with other folks. So if you work in an office, in your cubicle, no matter how solitary your work is, you can't stand to be alone forever.

We need human interaction. We need to feel connected to the larger world of our team, department, and organization.

> *We need this feedback because it helps us see how what we do fits in with the company as a whole*

It's in our DNA, don't you think? I imagine this goes back to Early Man at the beginning of time. How do you think Early Man would've felt if he came back to the camp and no one from the tribe was around?

"Hello... anyone here...? (Waits for answer; tries again.) Just slayed a Sabretooth tiger with one arrow, thank you very much! HELLO!... Gee, you think when you bring food back to the cave, SOMEBODY would be here to say, 'Nice job, Oog!'"

So, are you feeling *unplugged* from your work? Well, you have to roll up your sleeves and get to work. Here's how to reconnect with the big picture of your organization, and maybe reinvent your career in the process.

Oh, and yes, it will involve... brace yourself... doing some extra work:
- Read your company's annual reports, newsletters, and policy manuals.
- Ask to attend interdepartmental meetings to learn how other departments operate.
- Make friends and play nice with the folks inside and outside your department.
- Volunteer for interdepartmental committees and task forces.
- Find out how your company's products or services are viewed by its customers.

You should also build more connections within your own department. Here's how:
- Ask a coworker to help you on a project.
- Find a senior member of your department to mentor you.
- Communicate with your colleagues face-to-face as much as possible.
- Join the company softball team and bring beer. (Last part I made up, but it couldn't hurt.)
- Help or spearhead the next office social function.
- Figure out ways your department can work collaboratively with other departments.

PERSIST IN MAKING OUTSIDE CONNECTIONS
We've already discussed this in another chapter, but making connections outside the office is necessary for a successful career reboot. You can make connections in your professional community as well as your local community.

Here's how to connect with other professionals in your industry:
- Ask your manager and others who might be interested in your experience at your next industry networking event. If you get enough positive feedback, then offer to hold a brief meeting to share your expertise.
- Get a meeting buddy. Find out who else might already belong to, or want to join your industry's professional association, and plan on attending meetings together.
- Join the local chapter of your professional association.
- Ask your colleagues about any associations they might belong to that you haven't heard of.
- Ask your company to pay for it. If it isn't company policy, pay for the membership dues yourself, and check with your tax advisor or accountant, as it may be tax-deductible!

Reinvention Guy's Take-Away Tip: If you want to truly achieve something of significance in this world, you must also give something. Networking is no different.

Oh, sure, you can take in info, leads, and connections from other people for a while, but unfortunately, if they start to sense that you aren't giving anything back, that well will start drying up very quickly.

Here's some sure-fire ways to give back and keep those connections open.

- **Take immediate action.** When someone gives you a good piece of info, thank them immediately.
- **Chose the right people.** Network with others who can benefit from what you've learned.
- **Play close attention to the other person's needs.** Learn what your fellow networkers are interested in and when you come across some info they could use, share it with them.

Again, you can't wait on your boss to build those connections for you. You have to go out and create them on your own. Remember, if it's to be, it's up to you! Now go out there and connect.

IN REVIEW

Building connections means establishing relationships with others in your department, company, and industry. To form these links:

In Your Company:
- Read your company's annual reports, newsletters, and policy manuals.
- Ask to attend interdepartmental meetings to learn how other departments operate.
- Make friends with people inside and outside your department.
- Volunteer for interdepartmental committees and task forces.
- Find out how your company's products or services are viewed by its customers.

IN YOUR DEPARTMENT
- Ask a coworker to help you on a project.
- Find a senior member of your department to mentor you.
- Communicate with your colleagues face-to-face as much as possible.
- Join the company softball team.
- Help with the next office social function.
- Figure out ways your department can work collaboratively with other departments.

IN YOUR INDUSTRY
- Ask your manager and others who might be interested in your experience at a professional organization meeting. Offer to hold a brief meeting to share your findings.
- Get a meeting buddy.

▌Join the local chapter of your professional association.

▌Ask your colleagues about any associations they might belong to that you haven't heard of.

▌Ask your company to pay for it. If it isn't company policy, pay for the membership dues yourself.

GIVE AS MUCH AS YOU GET

▌When someone gives you a good piece of info, thank them immediately.

▌Network with others who can benefit from what you've learned.

▌Learn what your fellow networkers are interested in and when you come across some info they could use, share it with them.

Ever really think about what you want out of your career? I mean, do you really think about what makes you tick, and more importantly, why you even go to the same job every day?

In other words, do your values match up with your company's values? Not sure? Then turn the page and let's explore it together.

"The main requirements for this job are the ability to live without money, skilled at mind numbing work & getting along with disgruntled coworkers."

CHAPTER 23:

What Matters Most to You?
Determining your Values

"Work is an extension of personality. Is achievement. It is one of the ways in which a person defines himself, measures his worth — and his humanity."

— Peter Drucker

YOUR PERSONAL BOTTOM LINE

Let's face it, you want more from your work than just a paycheck. In this chapter, we'll explore our deepest reasons for showing up at work every day: our values.

Our values help us make decisions, simply because they outline what matters to us most.

Read that sentence again if you want. In fact, print it out and put it on your cubical wall, if you must. Now, that said, let's get back to You, Inc!

What matters most to you? What do you want out of work that you don't get from a paycheck? If you're like most people, you probably value stuff like:

▌ Friendly coworkers
▌ Creative, challenging work
▌ Freedom to do your work the way you want to do it
▌ A great boss

Do any of these sound like excellent reasons to come to work every day for the next thirty years? If so, they are probably in line with your values.

Hopefully, when our values match our work, we feel great. And when we feel great, our work feels meaningful and important.

But, when the work we do doesn't line up with our values, we feel that a certain *something* is missing. I'm sure you know what I am talking about. Things aren't quite right, even if you can't put your finger on why you feel a certain way.

Therefore, in this section, we're going to take a look at our values and how they affect our working lives.

DEFINE YOUR VALUES

To define what is most important to you, ask yourself questions like:

▌If you left your current job, what would you miss most?

▌What was the best job you ever had? Why?

▌When was the last time you felt truly energized at your job?

▌What value do you refuse to compromise on, no matter what?

Once again, think about the things that you value most. If you're getting those things, kudos. If not, make a commitment right now — starting today — that you will take steps to start getting them.

DEFINE YOUR EMPLOYER'S VALUES

Now, find out what your boss, team, and company value most.

To determine the boss's values:

▌Watch his actions. Is he a "Do as I say and not as I do" kind of guy, or not?

▌Notice when he praises you and what he praises you for.

▌Ask for his help in exploring your values and that of his and the company's. Tell him you are seeking ways to increase your own satisfaction on the job.

To determine your team's values:

▌**Talk to your team about their work values.** Ask them the same questions you asked yourself.

▌**Pay attention to their behaviors, attitudes.** Notice the activities that they enjoy, support, and discourage.

To determine the values of your company:

▌**Look for the unspoken cultural characteristics.** Does your company value fun? A work/life balance? Creativity? Its actions will tell you.

▌**Check the manual.** Look at what they say they value and reward versus what your experience has been. Do they say they value family, but you couldn't get the afternoon off to watch your daughter's softball game?

▌**Observe the behaviors of corporate leaders.** Is this behavior in line with published values or mission statements?

PUTTING IT TOGETHER

Once you know and understand your values and are pretty clear about theirs, it's time to line up any discrepancies.

Perhaps you value time with your family, and your company values 80 hour weeks without you seeing sunlight. If so, try to work on getting more of the specific time you value. What do you do next? Well, you go to your boss, or immediate supervisor, and discuss solutions like flextime or job sharing.

Don't forget: **A good manager knows that happy employees make better workers.** And if nothing gets solved, you can still look for what you need in other departments within the same company.

FOR THE BOSSES

As with any of this stuff, learning that your employees aren't exactly happy on the job is probably something most managers don't want to know about. But again, you can't just assume that everything is hunky dory because no one is complaining.

By actively engaging your employees and asking them questions, you can determine if their values are in line with yours and the company's.

So what kind of questions should you ask? As a group or individually, you should ask questions like:

▮ What do you look forward to the most at work?
▮ If you won the lottery, what would keep you from quitting your job?
▮ What would your ideal job be?
▮ When do you do your best work?
▮ What does success mean to you?

<u>**Reinvention Guy's Take-Away Tip**</u>: Once you have these answers, work on customizing the work for each of your staff. How? Simply match the job tasks of your employees with their values. Pretend your employees are your customers. Figure out what they value most and how best you can serve them.

Many managers automatically turn to money as the reason their employees stay. After all, it is a prime factor and easy to adjust. Again, it's worth repeating, it isn't the only factor.

Making employees stick around for years has more to do with the values of the organization — both yours and the company's. There is no getting around it: **If the three sets of values don't line up, sooner or later, your people will leave.**

IN REVIEW

How to determine what matters most to you.

● Determine your values by asking yourself questions about your ideal working environment.
● Determine the values of your boss, team, and company.

FOR THE BOSSES

Ask your employees if their job is in line with their values. Ask them:

- What do they look forward to the most at work?
- If they won the lottery, what would keep them from quitting their job?
- What is their ideal job?
- When do they do their best work?
- What does success mean to them?

Do you know your fellow workers? Oh, sure, you can go out and throw back some suds at the local watering hole, but do you really know their beliefs, wants, and needs?

A 22 year fresh-out-of-school newbie is going to look at life a whole lot differently than a 45 (twice divorced) male with child support whose been in the industry longer than the newbie's been alive.

Furthermore, you might find yourself sharing work with fellow workers that come from different generations. If so, then you should know where these folks are coming from.

Arming yourself with this knowledge will enable a smoother road to reinvention, and best of all, Chapter 24 gives you the insight to the different generations working today!

"I just don't get it. I've applied for over 200 jobs, but I've never even got a call back."

CHAPTER 24:

Bridging the Generation Gap

"Let us respect gray hairs, especially our own."

—J.P. Senn

Early Man realized that if he did NOT want to be eaten by a T-Rex, it might be prudent to team together with other like-minded Neanderthals. (The old safety in numbers scenario.)

Thus tribes were formed. And even though they worked for the betterment of all members of The Tribe, there was a pecking order to adhere to. Naturally, there were the *Young Guns* who, no doubt, had to answer to the Tribal Elders. For better or worse, it's the same today.

And if you are to successfully reboot your career, it's vital to know who your allies (and enemies) are in your tribal arena, aka *The Workplace*.

Let's pause and examine the four generations that you will most likely encounter every day in your cave. Having this information to draw upon will enable you to reach your goals faster and make these folks your allies.

SNAPSHOT OF THE MATURES

The Matures were born between 1909-1945. Here you get *2 for the price of 1* in generations. And that's because they are a combination of the Veterans (1901-1924) and the Silent Generation (1925-1942). Of the four generations still working today, *The Matures* are the smallest with only about 55 million people.

They are honored today by Tom Brokaw in the book, *The Greatest Generation* and in such films as *Saving Private Ryan*, *Band of Brothers*, and even on TV with *Mad Men*.

These folks lived through the Great Depression, Pearl Harbor, and helped take this country to impressive heights after WWII. Think of Jimmy Carter, John Glenn, Harrison Ford (yes, Luke Skywalker's bud), and John McCaine. As expected, they are courted by politicians because of their powerful lobbies, such as AARP.

IN THE WORKPLACE
∎ The Matures are people who are loyal to their employers and expect the same.
∎ They possess superb interpersonal skills.
∎ They enjoy flextime arrangements today — so they can work on their own schedule.
∎ They are *old school* in their thinking and believe promotions, raises, and recognition should come from job tenure.
∎ They measure their work ethic on productivity, timelines, and don't like to draw attention to themselves.
∎ They make the rules and follow them to a tee, because, well that's why they were established in the first place, for crying out loud! (Just visit any senior community in Florida and you'll know what I mean!)
∎ They don't like to rock the boat and believe the standard options are just fine, thank you, very much! (Give them a gas guzzling Buick and they're in heaven.)

SNAP SHOT OF BOOMERS
This is my generation, born between 1946–1964. When you think of this age group think, individuality, Me. No doubt about it, today *The Boomers* are definitely in control.

Need convincing? Then just look around and you'll notice they run our local, state, and national governments. They are usually the ones on TV asking their constituents and wives for forgiveness for breaking the vows of marriage. (See Elliot Spitzer, John Edwards, etc.) Love us or loathe us, baby, the Boomers are the bosses, supervisors, managers, and CEOs of most companies.

And yes, we dominate the workforce because of our enormous numbers. This generation is indeed dedicated to a solid, strong work ethic. This age group uniquely define themselves by taking pride and letting everyone around them (including their third cousin), know that they all work hard and long hours.

> "You young Generation X'ers … I have Popeye the Sailor Man Pez dispensers that are older than you. Look at me, me, me… working like a dog here, putting in fifteen hour days. Did I mention I am stressed, have prostate problems, and have high blood pressure?! HA! Top that!"

As you can plainly see, the word workaholics is easily attributed to the Boomers. Oh, did I mention that I am writing this chapter on a beautiful Saturday, which I should be enjoying right now, but because I HAVE a deadline looming I decided to sacrifice my weekend? (beat) Okay, just making sure you knew that!

Yes, Boomers take pride in burning the midnight oil and need face time with *The Boss*. If *The Matures* (their parents) built America's foundation after WWII into a major world player, then *The Boomers* (all 77 million of us, in the U.S.) have taken America (for better or worse) to a whole new level!

The formidable events in the Boomers' lives include: The Civil Rights Movement; John F. Kennedy's, Robert Kennedy's, and Martin Luther King's assassinations; and the Vietnam War! (Yep, let the good times roll.)

Of course, we also have Oprah Winfrey, Muhammad Ali, The Beatles, Bill Gates, Bill Clinton, and watching the dollar bill lose value!

Here are the *Top Ten Beliefs* of the Boomers...

- They evaluate themselves and others based on their work ethic.
- This same work ethic is yes, you guessed it, measured in hours worked.
- Teamwork is critical to success.
- Relationship building is very important.
- They expect loyalty from those they work with.
- They calculate productivity in those hours is less important.
- Technology brings with it as many problems as it provides a slew of solutions (Sonnova... my computer froze again!)
- Rules should be obeyed (unless they are contrary to what they want), then of course, they're to be broken. (How convenient!)
- They don't believe in taking sickies — why die at home when you can die at work and be recognized for your sacrifice?

And last, but certainly not least (drum roll please)... The # 1 belief of the Boomers is:

- They like to have LOADS of toys to show their peers, so they can say, "Look at me, I am so successful!" **

Except for their quirks and uptight, new age belief in the sacredness and importance of the individual and developing one's self into a more 'whole' person ... they're quite easy to get along with.

SNAPSHOT OF THE X'ERS
This age group was born between: 1965–1978. (Oh God, do I remember those years!) This generation is skeptical and were privy to experience Watergate, Fall of the Berlin Wall, the Challenger explosion, the Gulf War, the PC boom, the Reagan Presidency, Michael Dell and Monica Lewinsky.

(Unfortunately, they are too young to appreciate *The Ed Sullivan Show, Sonny and Cher Comedy Hour, or Starsky and Hutch*.)

For some unexplained reason, society (not me, of course) has labeled them as slackers. Yes, somehow, X'ers have been called unmotivated, lethargic, sarcastic, and irreverent.

This is not completely fair. Although if I were them, I'd be most chagrined that the only title of distinction I could get was just the letter X.

  Welcome to the world of Generation Brand X!

Call them unmotivated? Perhaps... but hey, you'd be too if your mom (probably a boomer) took *The Pill* possibly to not have you. This generation is not fond of military, church, and government, especially when most institutions (in their eyes, at least) have let them down.

The upside is that X'ers are much more laid-back than other generations.

- They avoid the hard-core, super-motivated, do or die Boomer work ethic.
- They want open communication regardless of position, title, or tenure.
- They **respect production** over tenure.
- They value control of their time.
- They invest in a particular person's loyalty, not a company.
- They can spot a phony a mile away.
- They want diversity and prefer options: plans B, C, and D (yes, even E, if there is one).
- They dig technology as a way to maintain control of their lives.

Now a major part of the workforce, X'ers have come to the conclusion that their company will not provide for them, that job security is an antiquated concept from their parent's generation (see *The Great Recession*), and it's no wonder they live their lives with a carpe diem attitude.

**http://www.marstoncomm.com/matures.html

And because they do, they focus on the short term to make sure each day has meaning. As Boomers enter into retirement (and become more like their own parents, gulp!), the X'ers can take solace in knowing that sooner than later, they'll be running The Show!

Yes! It's going to be their turn to get all the money, and of course, the debt that the Boomer generation left for them.

SNAP SHOT OF THE MILLENNIALS
This generation came of age between 1979–1988. Society, realizing how angry the X'ers were at only being identified with the third to last letter of the alphabet, decided not to screw up this time.

Resolute to make amends and give this coddled generation a full-figured description — Ladies and Gentleman, you know 'em, you love 'em, you certainly gave birth to 'em, please welcome, *The Millennials*.

These plucky young folk went through the Oklahoma City Bombing; 9/11 Terrorist Attack; the Internet boom; reality TV shows; Lindsay Lohan's and Britney Spear's rehab; Miley Cyrus; The Jonas Brothers; and LeAnn Rimes.

They are also at the forefront of the technology boom of cell phones, laptops, remote controls, YouTube, Facebook, MySpace... or plain just taking up space. They are, after all, the youngest of the generations.

Never truly knowing what life was without answering machines or slinkys, The Millennials live in a world omnipresent and overwhelmed with technology (which suits them just fine).

Studies reveal they will see more change in their lifetime than any other generation. When you get right down to it, the *Millennials* have really had it quite good, don't you think?

Except for that nasty little housing crisis from years back, their parents had money. So overall, they have experienced the greatest bull market in the history of mankind.

They are the soccer children of the battling soccer moms and dads. Sure, there is global terrorism with rogue countries trying to get nukes, global warming, green house gases, rising energy problems, and a whole slew of other problems.

But the good news is their parents did their best to insulate them from the big, old, nasty, cruel world and not ask for rent from them, like my folks did.

Unfortunately, times have changed. The Millennials have gotten older.

It's now time for them to leave the nest, enter the society as young adults, and take their rightful place in the workforce with a company that's hopefully not in Chapter 11.

You'll also notice there are a lot Millennials. Like rabbits, they're all over the place. So much so, that they rival the Boomers in size. All due, probably, to the procreating between the X'ers and the Boomers!

Unlike other previous generations, the Millennials actually like being led. And because they do, they are always looking for...

▌Individuals who will guide them toward achieving their goals.

▌They look to their supervisors and bosses for leadership.

▌They search for jobs that provide great, personal fulfillment and less stress in their lives.

▌They prefer open, constant communication and positive reinforcement from their boss.

▌Somehow, by the grace of God, they find working with *The Mature* generation pretty invigorating. (Go figure!)

How to Bridge the Gap & Change Your Viewpoint!

If the generation gap is making your work a bad place to be, try to bridge it before you cut bait and run to another company. You can:

▌**Get to know them better.** Talk to them about the good old days, so you can understand where they're coming from.

▌**Learn to see things from their perspective.** You might be very comfortable with using e-mail to do everything, but even you can recall when we didn't have e-mail. And your boss or colleague is still probably not used to it, or believes there are times when it isn't appropriate.

<u>Reinvention Guy's Take-Away Tip</u>: Sometimes, the attitudes we have about older or younger groups is to blame for our trouble getting along with these groups. Scientists call this **ageism**, which means discrimination against people because of their age. We might, for example, believe that old people are:

▌Slow or feebleminded

▌Close-minded, resistant to change

▌Out of touch

▌Afraid of change

On the other hand we might think young people are:

▌Disrespectful

▌Eager to disrupt the status quo

▌Ignorant or just plain dumb

But are these things the truth, or just what we've been conditioned to see by society? What if we changed those perceptions? What if we looked at an older person and instead saw:

▌Strong leaders

▌Knowledgeable sources of company history, wisdom, and patience

▌Someone who is committed and loyal to the firm

And what if instead of looking at a young person and seeing some upstart punk we saw:
▮ Determination
▮ An eagerness to learn
▮ The latest skills
▮ Fresh young minds that can help you solve problems
▮ New perspectives

...what then? How would your working relationships with these people change? Isn't it so much better than feeling that some Young Turk is after your job? Or that some senior Team Member is giving you the hairy eyeball for wanting to send him an e-mail?

Hopefully, you can understand that working side by side with people from different generations doesn't have to be a strain on you. By learning more about them and their backgrounds, understanding things from their point of view, and by accepting them for who they are, you can make your workplace a happier place.

IN REVIEW
There are four distinct generational groups working together today:
- Matures (1909-1945)
- Baby Boomers (1946-1964)
- Gen X'ers (1965 –1978)
- The Millennials (1979-1988)

To bridge the generation gap:
- Get to know the different age groups in your workplace better.
- Learn to see things from their viewpoint.
- Change your perspective about these age groups.

Whether you want to believe it or not, your co-worker can either help make or break your career. And no matter how much you kick and scream about it, their perception of you is their reality.

As you know, life is a chess match where you have to make the right moves and instinctively hope to know your adversaries' next moves. Well, office politics is no different.

Of course, you might not want to play the game, but sometimes, you have no choice. So, let's help you navigate those choppy seas to a more tranquil setting...

"Supply was out of harps."

CHAPTER 25:

Navigating the Choppy Seas of Office Politics

"Those who are too smart to engage in politics are punished by being governed by those who are dumber."

— **Plato** (Another Dead Philosopher)

"I don't participate in office politics," a woman said to me recently, sticking her nose in the air.

"Gee, that's too bad," I said. "Because your co-worker certainly are, and even when you're not playing the game, you can still get played."

Office politics is more common than most of us think. According to a survey conducted by California based staffing service, Office Team, U.S. executives said they waste 19% of their time — which amounts to about one day a week — dealing with company politics, including rivalries, internal conflicts, and other situations that can get pretty complex and even downright dirty.

So, here are a few pointers for navigating the complex web of intrigue and politics at your office:

REMEMBER: OFFICE POLITICS IS ABOUT THE POWER, BABY!

Every organization has a way to measure how much power its employees have. Some are tangible, like a company vehicle or other perk. Sometimes, it is simply perceived, like who has the nicest office. Your mission? Determine who has the most actual and/or perceived power in your office, and why.

One company that I worked for had an IT guy who thrived on keeping his power and hated anyone who got in his way when it came to making decisions about his domain — the computers. He knew if the system went down, the company was up the creek without a paddle.

Surprisingly, management got complaints about him butting heads with other employees, yet did nothing about it. Why? Well, in their narrow-mindedness they were afraid to fire him because of the computer passwords he had control over. In a nutshell, he could cripple their company. Yes, it's about the POWER! Wielding it, and keeping it!

LEARN FROM THE PAST

Here's where paying attention to office stories can help you more than reading the company's annual reports and newsletters.

Look for situations where the company has protected its upper management from things that would get you or anyone else fired, or maybe even arrested.

Noticing which colleagues aren't punished for incompetence or wrongdoing can tell you a lot about who wields the political power in your organization.

Don't Ignore the Office Grapevine (But Don't Believe Everything You Hear, Either!)

Yes, I've covered this a little already, but it really bears repeating: *The Grapevine* has its uses, but getting the facts isn't one of them.

However, it can be a source of good information that can lead you to the truth. You just have to dig deeper to get to the truth.

Again, in the long run, it pays to make friends with the people who nurture your office grapevine.

LOOK TO YOUR BOSS

"Part of everyone's job is learning how to make the boss look good," writes Alexandria Neely Martinez in an article on graduatingengineer.com.

A large part of fitting in is learning what your boss expects from you and constantly thinking up ways you can add more value to the company as a whole.

If you want to move up in the organization (which is part of what rebooting your career is all about), then knowing the answers to these questions will help make you more politically savvy, according to Martinez.

- Is your department a moneymaker for the company?
- Is your boss a team player?
- How is she perceived within the company?
- Does she have the power to make decisions that affect your goals?

Knowing the answers to these questions will help make you more valuable to your boss and the company, and even if you don't plan on actively engaging in office politics, you'll have a better idea of how the game is played in your company.

Rule #1 - When it comes to office politics, *don't make your boss look bad!*
Rule #2 - See RULE #1

REALIZE YOU HAVE OPTIONS
When you're the brunt of office politics, it's easy to feel cornered and helpless, but you're not. Yes, you may not be able to choose what happens to you all the time, but you can choose how you react to it.

Hopefully, when a coworker gets a promotion that should have been yours, or someone said something about you that isn't true, don't have an emotional outburst at work. (Do it in the parking lot, or wait until you get home and share it with your loved ones, like my father always seemed to do. But, I digress...)

TAKE YOUR TIME
Look, you can decide when, where, and how to react. But screaming at the offender at work five minutes after it happens isn't it.

TAKE IT OUTSIDE
Talk to a friend you don't work with, a family member, or your mentor about what happened. Ask for their suggestions about what you should do. Whatever you do, I beg you *do NOT vent to your fellow employees.*

Take it from me, they may be your friends, but as sure as the sun rises in the east, they might be even better friends with the person who slighted you.

Oh, and now the plot thickens. Your confidante may also be after the same positions and perks that you want. It gets worse. Your co-worker pal could very well be in a position to use something you've told them against you for leverage to get what they want.

ABOVE ALL STAY POSITIVE AND FLEXIBLE
Grinning and bearing it through a tough situation will send the message to your boss that you are adaptable to change, a good long-term career trait.

Trust me on this. Bitching and moaning will not help. While you shouldn't just bottle everything up inside, choosing a more appropriate time and place to vent your frustrations will allow you to stay your usual professional self.

DON'T MAKE IT PERSONAL
Yes, this is the hardest part, because our work is often very personal to us. Try to remember that it isn't always about you (even when it is about you). When you're politically attacked at work, it could just mean that someone else feels threatened by you. Yes, I know. For some oddball reason unrelated to your job, or the power they perceive

you as wielding, they have it in for you.

KEEP YOUR EYES AND EARS OPEN; YOUR MOUTH CLOSED

Actually, that's good marriage advice too, but of course, that's another book. Keeping your eyes and ears open and your mouth closed simply means being careful who you associate with at work.

Connecting with a certain group is natural, especially if you're just starting a new job. It helps you get acclimated to the corporate culture and adjust and make friends. Just make sure you aren't connecting with the wrong group. Common sense dictates that you be friendly with everybody and get the full range of personalities and opinions at work.

You'll notice that most of these rules are less about the office politics of other people and more about you, and there's a reason for that. **At the end of the day, you are the only person you have any control over.**

Below are a few other rules, courtesy of Jamie Fabian, writing for JobCircle.com:
- **Focus on what you need to achieve.** Figure out what you want at work and plan your strategy for getting it.
- **Get out in the market place.** Be a part of more than one network and communicate with them often.
- **Study Success.** Watch peak-performing people at work, and do what they do.
- **Take the high-road at work.** Don't pass judgment or spread rumors.
- **Make it a win-win.** Look for ways to solve conflicts where everyone benefits.

KEEP YOUR FRIENDS CLOSE; YOUR ENEMIES CLOSER

In the end, the above advice comes down to a line from *The Godfather*. Sonny (Al Pacino) Corleone turns to Fredo, his brother, and says, "Keep your friends close, and your enemies closer."

This is a very good mantra to go by in life and in business. **Especially in business**. Of course, I don't want you to feel too paranoid right now. Okay, maybe a little. But in fact, you should be.

Here's why. How well do you really know your co-workers? Honestly, do you think of them as your friends first, or just someone you can hang with during work? More importantly, can you trust them with your innermost secrets? If not, then I wouldn't. When in doubt, leave them out (of your loop!)

When dealing with people I try to keep an open mind and do my best to sum up people, whenever I can. (Friend or foe?) And yes, at times I wear my heart on my sleeve with folks I deem friends.

But this is about you and your situation, isn't it? So ask yourself:

■ Can you trust your fellow workers with the news that you are dissatisfied with the status quo?

■ Can you reveal to them that you're working on getting a raise or a promotion, or transferring to another department?

My experience has shown me that for the most part people are gossips. And because they are, it's prudent to keep your career aspirations close to your vest!

Make no mistake, everyone thinks about #1… and friends or not, they might not want you succeeding over them, no matter how much they say they have your back. Just something to think about as you go about rebooting your career.

ACT WITH INTEGRITY
Hopefully, you're not looking at office politics through rose-colored glasses. But at the end of the day, the best way to deal with office politics is with integrity, honesty, and by keeping your company's objectives at heart.

If you find yourself on the receiving end of an attack, try NOT to stoop to your attacker's level.

And if you're a team leader, let each member know that any game playing won't be tolerated. Sure, it won't make your time at work any easier, but at least you'll navigate the minefield of office politics and still be able to sleep at night.

KNOW THE TYPES
Here's the part that I love to discuss. You see, every office has — how do I say this nicely — a wide variety of people from all different backgrounds.

Many of these folks fall under different personality types. For fun (yours), I've identified a few such types that I've come across in my travels that may be lurking around your office. As you read through the list, you'll no doubt think of a few of your own. Here goes:

THE DRAMA QUEEN (OR KING)
Some people's lives are full of drama, and this spills over into their professional lives. (I am sure you know these people.) So, do you work with someone who has to leave suddenly due to some emergency, only everything that happens to them seems to be an emergency?

Their friend's cat died. Baskin-Robbins stopped making their favorite ice cream flavor. Their car and washing machine spontaneously burst into flames during the family's weekend barbecue.

The Drama Queen or King is the *Master of Disaster*. Everything, no matter how major or minor, is grounds for them to whine all day. Usually they call in sick and generally act like basket cases.

THE OFFICE CRAB
The office crab criticizes everyone and everything. Somehow, this person never seems to be a Happy Camper. Not surprisingly, he or she accomplishes very little. The one skill that they have mastered, somehow, by the grace of God, is they have the innate ability to suck the positive energy out of the room, along with the creativity of the team.

In essence, The Crab makes everyone as miserable as they are. Rumor has it she is the first cousin to The Drama Queen, or in reality, is the Drama Queen in disguise!

YE OLDE SUCK UP
This worker thinks the only way to move up is by schmoozing up to the boss. And heck, in some companies, Ye Olde Suck Up might be right! You see, he or she has achieved a level of power at your firm that no one else believes he or she deserves. Alas, Ye Olde Suck Up has mastered the art of butt kissing and there's nothing you can do about it.

Sure, you can have a sign on your desk saying, **"You are now in a NON-Kiss Ass Zone!"** and you can refuse to hang out with them, but you have to play nice, especially if Ye Olde Suck Up is your immediate supervisor.

THE GOSSIP
The office gossip loves to hear and dish dirt on everyone in the organization. The upside to all of this is that The Gossip can be a source of useful info. It's best, though, to try and verify what he or she tells you before you act on it.

BUT whatever you do, do NOT, and I repeat, do NOT tell The Gossip that you're fed up with your job and looking for a change.

As surely as Lindsay Lohan's bail bondsman is on her speed dial, word will get back to your boss before your next coffee break. Oh, and trust me, the gossip on you will have more embellishments than the show Celebrity Rehab to make the story even better.

THE BUSYBODY
You know 'em, you love 'em, but you can't get 'em out of your hair. I'm talking about the fellow worker who is always in everyone's business. Like a true co-dependent, they seem to thrive on knowing everything they can about your personal life, what projects you're working on, blah, blah, blah...

Worst of all, they always have one ear to the ground, listening for whispers or mentioning of their name. Usually this person is best friends with the Office Gossip, or in the world of two-for-the price of one, are in fact the same person.

THE VICTIM

I love listening to the Victim, why? Because deep down I am content that I am NOT that person. For some strange reason, everything seems to happen to The Victim. And of course, it's never, ever, their fault, right?

Their life is an episode of the *Jerry Springer Show* with The Law of Misfortune following them like a dog noticing a treat in their back pocket.

God bless the Victim. They attract calamity and blame the world for everything bad that befalls them. Oh, and if you've jumped ahead, yes, Victim and the Drama Queen (or King) can even be one and the same.

<u>Reinvention Guy's Take-Away Tip</u>: For better or worse — and whether we want to admit it — we are ALL these cast of characters at one time or another. Hell, you, who are reading this, might in fact be The Victim, but you don't see yourself as it.

The Busy Body listens to The Victim, turns away, then becomes Gossip Girl, and quicker than you can say Sarah Palin, NEW gossip has been launched.

How do these characters affect your reinvention? Here's how: Office politics are inevitable in any organization. So, whether you play or not, keep these tips in mind and you'll have a long and happy career at your current company without jumping ship to another firm.

IN REVIEW

▐ Remember that it's all about power.
▐ Learn from the company's past about what to do now.
▐ Don't ignore the office grapevine, it could be your pipeline to gathering much needed information about what is going on.
▐ Look to your boss for clues about what is going on at the company.
▐ Realize you have options (even when the going gets tough at your job).
▐ Take your time, make prudent and smart moves that can boost your value to your company.
▐ Take it outside.
▐ Stay positive as best you can.
▐ Don't make it personal.
▐ Keep your eyes and ears open; your mouth closed.
▐ Keep your friends close; your enemies closer.
▐ Act with integrity.

There is one talent that everyone possesses, but somehow over the years, for one reason or another, we suppress it. Every child has this talent and uses it every day with remarkable results.

Unfortunately, as we get older we lose touch with it. And that's too bad, because if you want peace and tranquility in your career... if you want to be healthy, wealthy, and wise in your professional and personal life... you have to have this one thing working for you.

Having it will enable you to get through the challenging times you will face. Having this facility costs nothing, and yet, it can keep giving back to you over and over again.

Research has shown it can lower your blood pressure and help boost the quality of your life. Best of all, once you possess this talent, no one can ever take it away from you.

To learn how best to use This Secret go on to the next chapter.

An Industrial Inferiority Complex

CHAPTER 26:
Finding the Humor in Your Job

"Do not take life too seriously.
You will never get out of it alive."

— **Elbert Hubbard**

Throughout this book, we've covered some serious subjects, albeit in what I hope has been a somewhat humorous way.

However, to really stick with the changes you want and need to make in your career, you need to maintain your sense of humor — about yourself and your work.

In regards to my personal and professional life, I realized a long time ago that if I wanted to not only survive, but thrive, the one aspect that I had control of... the one thing that helped me keep my sanity... the one thing that NO charlatan, tormenting officer worker, or boss could ever take away from me was — my sense of humor!

A daily dose of humor and the laughter that goes a long with it is vital to your physical and mental health. How so? Well, did you know...

- Every time you have a good hearty laugh (for about 10 minutes), you burn up 3-1/2 calories?
- Laughing increases oxygen intake and that replenishes and invigorates cells. In addition, it also increases the pain threshold, boosts immunity, and relieves stress.
- The average pre-schooler smiles or laughs around 400 times a day. Worse, that number drops to only 15 times a day by the time people reach age 35. (Gulp?! What happens when you reach 50?)
- People smile only 35 percent as much as they think they do?
- Laughter releases endorphins. This chemical is 10 times more potent than the pain-relieving drug morphine, with the same exhilarating effect as doing strenuous exercise.

Depending upon your attitudes towards your boss and co-workers, cubicles can be boring, life-sucking prisons, or a place you can't wait to get to every day.

I remember in my office, I had a framed family portrait on my desk. There was the wife, kids, the big collie with the youngest child giggling and hugging the pooch. The inscription read:

"Daddy, we love you!"

Yes, the perfect picture of contentment. My co-workers would walk by and comment on it. In fact, one day, another employee, let's call her Susan (because that's her name), passed by my desk and said,

> "Wow, what a lovely portrait... your wife is stunning, and those kids... you want to just eat them up, they're adorable! What are their names?"

I replied,

> "Wish I knew... they're someone else's family, not mine. I am single, but if I was to have a wife and kids, I'd like for them to look just like that."

All of a sudden, Susan broke out LAUGHING and called over other co-workers to check out Peter's (my) faux family gathering.

Everyone loved it. They couldn't believe that I would place a bogus family portrait on my desk. I said,

> "Look, you all have family photos of your significant (or 'insignificant' other)... I didn't want to feel left out... Am I NOT allowed to have the same happiness?"

This made the other workers in my office LAUGH even more. In fact, every few months, I'd put up ALL new photos of other families and Photoshop my face onto the face of the father in the picture.

I am proud to say this became a running gag in the office. The more outrageous the photos, the more my contemporaries LOVED the fact I was making up a life for myself to fit in.

What does this all mean to you? It means, it's important to inject (as best you can) a sense of fun, loads of laughter, and playfulness into what would otherwise be a boring, stressful, sterile, and very un-fun place, *The Office!*

Laughter and humor are integral to a more productive environment. Just imagine, creating a fun daily work life will help:

- break up boredom and fatigue
- fulfill human social needs
- break up conflict and communication

∎ fulfill the need for mastery and control (Bob, would you please just LET it go!)
∎ improve communication

How important is laughter to your mental health (at home and at work)? A survey by Hodge-Cronin & Associates found that of 737 CEOs surveyed, 98 percent preferred job candidates with a sense of humor to those without.

Further research indicated that 84 percent of the executives thought that employees with a sense of humor do a better job than people with little or no sense of humor.

Now, you may not know this, but humor studies have been done on this subject.

Dr. David Abramis at California State, Long Beach, studied fun at work for years and discovered that workers who have fun on the job are more productive, more creative, better decision-makers, and get along better with co-workers.

And if you're in HR this should interest you: FUN employees have fewer absentees, late and sick days than people who aren't having fun.

BECOME THE CCO (CHIEF COMICAL OFFICER)
If your company doesn't have one (some do!), appoint yourself as your company's Chief Comical Officer. Think of some clever, funny, and creative ways to liven up your boring workday. Here are a few ideas to get you started. You could:

∎ Decorate the employee bathrooms with decorative knickknacks and humorous wall art.
∎ Decorate your boss's or coworker's office or cubicle for their birthday.
∎ Talk the boss into throwing in on a little company picnic for your department.
∎ Engage in a little friendly verbal sparring with colleagues.
∎ Tell jokes (appropriate ones, of course).

The sky's the limit! Small, low, or no cost activities can increase the levity index at your firm.

FOR THE BOSSES
The benefits of a pleasant and happy workplace are numerous. Happy employees are more loyal and more productive. There is less absenteeism and a lower tardiness rate. Why? Well, I believe when people have a fun environment, they look FORWARD to work.

And I am sure no one has to tell you that STRESS is a killer (both personally and professionally)!

The turnover rate may decrease, as employees feel content and loyal to an organization, and the cost associated with illness may decrease as people experience the positive physiological and psychological effects of laughter.

Can you, as a boss, measure the results of fun and laughter in your workplace? Sure. Look who is calling in sick all the time... look at your turnover rates pre-FUN and LAUGHTER program implementation.

Look at it this way — creating a more fun-filled atmosphere could very well create HAPPIER employees. And guess what? Happier employees could very well decrease customer complaints.

What does this mean to you as the boss or immediate supervisor? It means you have a lot of control over the work environment. Will it be one of dour seriousness, or fun? The choice is yours. Yes, I know, if you're old school, you're thinking,

> "I don't have time for FUN! We have a business to run here. It's called WORK for a reason!"

In fact, you may be one of those bosses who think fun has no place at work. You might believe that you can't be both professional and fun at the same time.

Worse, your perception is that you have to plan for fun, or that having fun at work will lower your department's results, and negatively affect the company's bottom line.

Well, my non-believer, if this chapter teaches us anything, it's that this couldn't be further from the truth.

One way to keep your best people is by creating and supporting a fun working environment. No one likes to be stuffy, dour, and serious all the time. You can lighten the mood without lightening the productivity. Here's how:

- Hire employees who already value fun and have a sense of humor.
- Make sure humor is modeled by you and upper management.
- Set up a Fun Committee. Let your employees participate and come up with fun things to do around the office.
- Encourage spontaneity.
- Celebrating employees' birthdays in unique, special ways.
- Wear a silly or offbeat tie to work.
- Let employees dress up for Halloween, and you do so, as well.

<u>Reinvention Guy's Take-Away Tip</u>: Having fun at work doesn't mean disruption, spending money, or not getting the job done. Bear in mind, having fun at work, or creating a sense of playfulness, means breeding creativity and innovation in your department, de-stressing, and making sure your Super-Star players stay right where they are.

IN REVIEW
Having fun at work doesn't mean you have to spend a lot of money, or that your team's productivity will decline. Let's surmise, to have more fun at work:

- Decorate the employee bathrooms with decorative knickknacks and humorous wall art. (Let them take an active part of this.)
- Decorate your boss's or coworker's office or cubicle for their birthday.
- Talk the boss into throwing in on a little company picnic for your department.
- Engage in a little friendly verbal sparring with colleagues.
- Tell jokes (appropriate ones, of course).

FOR THE BOSSES
- Hire employees who already value fun and have a sense of humor.
- Make sure humor is modeled by you and upper management.
- Set up a Fun Committee. Let your employees participate and come up with fun things to do around the office.
- Encourage spontaneity with yourself and colleagues.
- Celebrating employees' birthdays in unique, special ways.
- Wear a silly or offbeat tie to work.
- Let employees dress up for Halloween, and you do so, as well.

I cannot stress this enough: *Morale is a very important part of having a good work/life balance.* Taking the time to infuse a sense of fun and acknowledging your fellow colleagues — the fuel that runs your company — is quite important.

Your company then becomes family. And as everyone knows, family is everything... except when somebody dies and everyone goes after the money in the estate. (But THAT, my friend, is a whole other book that I will write some day.)

Want to know a way to help you reach your goals? Well, it has nothing to do with mastermind groups, or networking. No, it really has to do with developing a mindset to accomplish your goals.

It helped Chuck Norris become a star... it helped me reinvent myself. Have it and it can toughen you up for overcoming challenges that work and life throw at you.

CHAPTER 27:

How a "Black Belt Mindset" Can Help Reboot Your Career!

"He who hesitates, meditates in a horizontal position"

—Senior Grand Master Ed Parker / Kenpo Karate

I love the above saying, which was first said by the late Senior Grand Master, Ed Parker, the founder of American Kenpo karate, a modern, scientifically developed martial art system that has its roots in China and developed in Hawaii.

It was then brought to the mainland by Grand Master Parker. Elvis Presley was a proponent and practitioner of Kenpo, as well as many other celebrities, like Sidney Poitier and Robert Culp.

Let's examine what the Parkism means. It means when facing an attack, if you hesitate (or you're not sure about which technique to land when battling an opponent), that split second of indecision could cost you your life!

Just like in business, we also have split-second decisions to make. Such as when an opportunity is presented to us, do we accept it? Or lament later on that we let it slip through our fingers?

I'm sure nobody has to tell you that the right decision can open doors you never thought existed. The wrong one, yes... could cost you career advancement down the road.

In martial arts as well as in business and life, we are called upon to make decisions that can affect ourselves, our family, and our co-workers.

There is a physical as well as spiritual part of the martial arts. It not only gives us strength, confidence, channels aggression, improves our overall health (cardio as well as helps us drop those nasty pounds), it gives us the tools to battle the urban mean streets environment we live in. Not only that, but...

Practicing and then mastering the martial arts also gives us the necessary tools to battle what could be our toughest opponent... ourselves!

HOW A "BLACK BELT MINDSET" CAN HELP REBOOT YOUR CAREER!

What everyone strives for in martial arts (at least I did) is to get a black belt.

That's because a black belt announces to lower belts (white through brown) that you've arrived. In the business world it would equate to a large promotion and new status at your company.

What does this mean for you? It means that when it comes to self-improvement and reaching one's goals, having a *Black Belt Mindset* can, undoubtedly, help you successfully reboot your career.

Best of all, it can help install a discipline within yourself that tells you, in your gut, what you KNOW needs to be done to tackle and accomplish your goals!

I began my study of the martial arts in my twenties in Shoto-Kan. A Japanese, traditional style. Then in my thirties, I switched to Kenpo, a complex martial art which has about a hundred and fifty base moves.

Eventually, in my early 40's, I went on to earn a first degree, then a second degree black belt. I even placed third in a kata (forms) competition at a Karate tournament. (And in case you're wondering, no, there were more than three participants.)

Of course, depending upon your body's conditioning, the later you begin to master any physical activity, the more challenging it becomes. The martial arts are certainly no different.

You have to get your body to do things that would be so much easier to accomplish in your youth, such as stretching and gaining flexibility.

Of course, while your body is more limber in your youth, you might not appreciate what you have until you have trouble doing it later on.

The beauty of getting older (and wiser) is that when you work more efficiently to gain a black belt and the *Black Belt Mindset*, you truly appreciate what you've accomplished.

In the real world, having a *Black Belt Mindset* allows you to diffuse an altercation before it escalates to violence. If there is no way out, a Black Belt Mindset allows you to deliver a series of devastating blows to your opponent.

The good news is you can acquire a *Black Belt Mindset* without ever having to put on a gi (white karate uniform) or learning the martial arts. Training yourself to have one will absolutely help you successfully reinvent your career. That's because...

Having a Black Belt Mindset During Your Reinvention...

▮ Will allow you to center yourself and get clear on what you have to achieve within your career.

▮ Will allow you to admit flaws that have blocked your growth and then give you the motivation to improve upon them.

▮ Will allow you to dig deep to discover how you can help others, as well as yourself, reach goals at your company.

▮ Will give you the energy and foresight to deliver value to your employer, yourself, and your clients.

▮ Will give you the knowledge that there are always options to consider before taking drastic action.

▮ Will give you the discipline to learn a new and valuable skill that will permit you to leap over your competitors.

▮ Tells you that your journey never ends and that you are open to improving yourself every day.

▮ Will allow you to push yourself out of your comfort zone to do what is necessary to reach Star or Superstar status at your company!

During your reinvention (and just like the martial arts), your journey begins as a white belt. As you progress, you then begin to take the necessary actions (small steps) that will help propel you forward to achieving your goals.

Yes, there will be challenges. One step forward... two steps back. It's part of the process! In the martial arts, it's learning new katas, weapons training, self-defense moves, etc.

In the business world, it's learning how to deal with some flaws that are holding you back... dealing with office politics... promotion going to someone else... hearing "NO" from your superiors.

Thankfully, through diligence and discipline, your reinvention skill level goes from white belt up to black belt with your muscle memory remembering the moves you need to get the job done!

And when they do, every movement becomes second nature. As a beginner, your moves are *herky-jerky*. As you improve, they begin to flow effortlessly like water over rocks.

A martial artist with a *Black Belt Mindset* knows the damage he can inflict on an enemy, but does his best to diffuse a situation before taking out his enemy!

In your career, having a *Black Belt Mindset* will give you the tools to zig while others zag. You will see the insurmountable odds in front of you as a unique opportunity to succeed.

Sure, others might throw in the proverbial towel at these challenges, but you will figure out other moves to get what you want!

In a nutshell: **A Black Belt Mindset gives you the will to persevere over barriers that get in your path.**

The plain truth is this: When you decide the path to reinvention, you WILL be tested by others to see if you've got the goods. But you will... you will have the strength, or Eye of the Tiger, as well as the Wisdom of the Dragon.

Empty Your Cup... Then Fill It Up with New Knowledge!

In the martial arts there is a term called *emptying your cup*. This means that you do NOT judge new ideas that are presented to you.

The beauty in all this is when you reinvent yourself, you are NOT giving up all you know. Your past experiences are great teachers. *This is a part of you.* In emptying your cup with this scenario, you are adding NEW knowledge to your databank.

In emptying your cup, you should NOT judge what you are being taught, but just do it. Later on, hopefully, the method in this madness will all make sense to you.

For instance, when the character, Mr. Miyagi in *The Karate Kid* asked Danielson (played by actor, Ralph Macchio) to do certain chores or tasks, it confused Danielson as he couldn't understand why washing a car was going to make him a better fighter. (Remember wax on... wax off?)

What Danielson's mentor/teacher was showing him was doing certain movements over and over again (regardless of how boring they were) would enable the actions to become second nature to him.

During your reinvention you might be asked by your mentor to do certain things that might be confusing or alien to you. That's expected. Do it anyway. (If they're aligned with your values). Oh, and what you might not know is that...

A mentor (or instructor) is getting as much as he is giving to you.

When I reinvented myself into a new career, I decided to learn an in-demand, financially in-demand skill. I chose copywriting (or sales writing).

In the beginning of my journey, one of my mentors, and a teacher of master copywriters, instructed his students to type out (and print out in long hand) other world class sales letters over and over again.

Why? Because doing so would help build our brain neurons to understanding what powerful copywriting felt like.

Internalizing this type of writing allows you to exponentially build your skill level. **Remember, to master a new skill or to improve your mindset, repetition will always be the key.**

Martial Artist, Jim Bouchard of thinklikeablackbelt.org sums it up best:

> "The mindset of the Black Belt Master is really a 'Beginner's Mind.' Instead of being satisfied with the status quo, the Master approaches each day with a sense of wonder and authentic curiosity — what can I learn and improve today? Ironically, the novice is usually not aware of this powerful mindset. Your mind must be tempered by experience and wisdom to become aware of the process of learning that we call 'Beginner's Mind'. Once you're aware of this process, it becomes a powerful tool for continual self-improvement, discovery and adventure! Perfection is not a destination, it's a never-ending process... Enjoy!"

<u>**Reinvention Guy's Take-Away Tip**</u>: While training in Kenpo karate, I realized there would be no short-cuts to getting awarded a black-belt. You had to earn it!

Career Reinvention is the same. You don't want to be a one hit wonder do you? Well, then, you should do your best to build a strong foundation to your career.

A Black belt Mindset will give you the stamina to persevere... to get out of your comfort zone and to do things that aren't necessarily easy at first, but once tackled correctly, they will be!

Remember (and forgive me for sounding all new-age and motivational here), what you put into your reinvention you will receive back tenfold.

Training yourself to have a *Black Belt Mindset* is your secret weapon to getting Star or Superstar status at your company, if that is your goal! And even if that is a lofty achievement, you can still use it to find fulfillment!

REVIEW
■ Do what you can to create a *Black Belt Mindset*
■ Get clear on what you really want out of your job and career

▌Trust your instincts
▌Get out of your comfort zone
▌Discover what you can to help you and your fellow co-workers
▌Empty your cup and accept new knowledge
▌Discipline yourself to learn a new and valuable skill that can help your company

Let's do a mini recap: You got a mentor... created a contribution statement... you dotted your I's and crossed your T's. In addition, you put in the time to create an effective synergy between you, your co-workers, and company. Unfortunately, with all your good intentions, things don't always work out the way you envisioned.

Again, don be too concerned. I call this the *it is what it is* syndrome! It may not be your fault, and it may be your good intentions were not taken to heart by The Powers That Be! (And you know who they are.)

So, what do you do next when you've exhausted all avenues to getting what you want at work with very little return on your investment? Well, the last chapter tells you what you know in your heart you have to do.

I believe Bill Cosby sums it up best: "I don't know the key to success, but the key to failure is trying to please everybody!"

God on the fifth day.

CHAPTER 28:

Hello, I Must Be Going...

"When the going gets weird, the weird turn pro."

—Hunter S. Thompson

You're at the point in your career where you've tried everything in this book, and yet, your current situation still isn't any better.

And because you're NOT happy with the status quo, you decide to pull up stakes and go to greener pastures. It happens, and because it does, rest easy in knowing you gave it your best shot.

There's no fault in deciding when to hold 'em, and when to fold 'em and just walk away.

Hold the phone a second. Before you exit stage right, make sure that what you are going to really is better than what you are leaving. In this section, we are going to look at doing just that and learn how to depart the right way.

THINK BEFORE YOU LEAP

You may know exactly what you want in your next job, but if not, you need to figure it out. Think about:

- The kind of work you want to do.
- The type of company you want to do it for.
- The kind of boss and work environment you are seeking.
- The things that matter the most to you. Is it money? Or do you seek challenges, creativity, and the chance to learn new things?
- How long will it take you to replace what you had in terms of your reputation, skill level, and relationships with customers and your fellow employees?
- How much money will you leave behind from your retirement plan, 401(k), salary, bonuses, and insurance?

INVESTIGATE

If you are considering a move to another company, or they've already offered you a job, then start doing some detective work. Here are a few suggestions. They'll take some work and time, but they are more than worth it in terms of the things you'll learn.

- **Ask if it's acceptable to talk to your future colleagues.** Ask them about the work, the company, the boss, and the culture. Do they love their work and the company they work for? Or do they hate it as much as you hate your current employer.
- **If possible, hang out in the parking lot of the new company early in the morning and at quitting time.** How many people arrive at daybreak and stay long after sundown? How happy, vibrant, or run down do people look as they arrive? When they leave?
- **Check out their website.** If your potential employer is a publicly held company, it will publish an annual report. Download it and read it. And check blogs, forums, and other sites for what customers and former employees are saying about the company.

HOW TO LEAVE THE RIGHT WAY

Now that you've accepted a great new job with your new dream company, it's time to hand in your notice. But there's a right way and a wrong way to do this.

Since you're reading this book, you've no doubt ran all sorts of revenge fantasies through your head for the day you finally leave your job, but playing out these scenarios in real life can be damaging to your new career.

Especially the ones that end with a SWAT team and news helicopters circling the building. Therefore, here are a few expert tips for quitting your old job safe and sound:

1. ANNOUNCE YOUR RESIGNATION

Type up a formal letter of resignation and hand deliver it to your boss. Don't e-mail or phone it in. Don't tell her you're leaving because she's a sorry SOB and her company sucks. Just tell her that you need to move on and thank her for her time and everything she's done for you (even if all she did was make you completely miserable and you built a voodoo doll in her likeness).

2. TELL YOUR IMMEDIATE SUPERVISOR FIRST

Don't tell any of your colleagues that you are leaving until you have told your direct supervisor. This sends him the message that you respect him. Remember that this is the person most likely to give a great reference for you to your next and any future employer.

3. DON'T SLACK OFF

A lot of people want to slack off as soon as they've turned in their two week's notice, happily riding the clock until their last day. This sends a bad message about your work ethic and can even undo all your years of hard work. You don't want news of your laziness getting back to your new employer.

<u>Reinvention Guy's Take-Away Tip</u>: **Don't rub it in**. Don't gloat to your supervisors and colleagues that you can't wait to get out of there and how the new company is so much better. Truth be told, no one wants to hear that. If they ask you where you're going, tell them, but don't add embellishments. You'll only make them hostile towards you, and who needs that, even for two weeks?

IN REVIEW

- Think before you leap
- Investigate all opportunities
- Announce your resignation
- Tell your immediate supervisor first
- Don't slack off
- Don't rub it in

There you go. Some simple steps on how to leave the right way. Now go, Grasshopper. Fly into your new life and new career. I hope you make the most of it. Before you close this book, I want to share a few insights that you will find useful during your reboot.

Yes, I know my book contains twenty-seven ways to reboot your career, but because you've been a swell reader I decided to give you some extra tips and techniques to tinker around with during your reinvention.

Discovering "The Role" You Play in Your Reinvention

"When we are no longer able to change a situation,
we are challenged to change ourselves."

—Victor Frankl

I wanted to leave you with some ideas to ponder as you begin your journey. And yes, reinvention is a journey. No doubt, you will have your challenges... triumphs... and everything in between.

Most of all, during this time, you will experience self-reflection — past and present — on how you approach co-workers, bosses, and yes, even family and friends who will, hopefully, be supportive and help you reach your goals.

Make no mistake: No one ever becomes successful in their careers without assistance from others.

That said, one of the most important aspects of your reinvention, and one that'll make yours go smoother, is if you notice the roles you play through life. About now, you might be thinking to yourself,

"I am NOT who I am? Now, I am playing a role?"

Fortunately, we all do. And whether we ever want to admit it or not, just like characters in a movie or play, we portray different attitudes and react differently to different stimuli from different people.

Understanding this concept is vital, because it will help you master the art of persuasion. And persuasion is a much needed skill to have if you want to go from point A to point B in your career.

I am not talking about manipulation. I'm talking about learning the skill of persuasion that helps others see your point of view. Once they do, you'll see how faster and more efficiently you can get that promotion, your baby (aka project) off the ground, etc.

And here's another good example of what I mean in regards to role playing. A few years back there was an excellent HBO movie called *The Life and Death of Peter Sellers*, staring Jeffrey Rush. It was a fun and introspective look at the comic genius.

In this film we see Sellers *transforming* himself through his journey to movie stardom. The man slipped into a new role as easily as you or I would slip into a pair of gloves. Remarkably, at times, you never knew where the real Peter Sellers ended and the character began.

In each scene of the movie, we saw Peter Sellers reinventing himself as he was dealing with his own demons as well as the studio heads and producers that awarded him his roles. (Notice how I used demons and Hollywood producers in the same sentence. Coincidence? I think not!)

It seems throughout his life, Peter Sellers was always reinventing himself for each role successfully. Well, reinvention can deliver the same results. The beauty of reinvention is that is allows you to shed your old skin and prosper with more purpose and control over your future.

Once you seriously go onto rebooting your career, you can alter the perception society (your colleagues, bosses, friends, etc.) has about you. But to do that, you have to take stock in...

The Characters YOU Play Daily

For instance, notice the way you act toward your boss, your colleagues, and your spouse. You are always having to zig then zag to persuade them to give you what you want,or to accept you.

Ever notice that how you act with an old college chum is different then, say, when you're with your daughter? *Your history with people dictates your behavior with them.*

Though you've certainly changed over the years, your buddy still remembers you as the guy who woke up naked with a hangover on the football field just as the marching band started practicing. (And no... that never happened to me... ever ... not once!)

But know this... If you are going to reinvent yourself into a new career and new life, you might have to change the roles people now expect you to play.

New Career, New Beginning... or Is It?

Dan Kennedy, an uber successful marketer and copywriter, points out that we get comfortable in the roles we play every day. And though we might be unhappy with the way our life is going, the fear and trauma of stepping outside and changing our characters is worse than the pain of continuing to play them.

In other words, we feel comfortable in our own uncomfortable skin. We sometimes look at bad situations through rose-colored glasses...'cause it's easier that way.

Dan reveals four self-defeating roles that people tend to perform to perfection.

The Victim (a.k.a. the Whiner): "Why me? Why is life sooooo unfair?"
The Martyr: "I gave up EVERYTHING for you!"
The Last Angry Man: "I'm mad as hell at everybody and everything!"
The Misunderstood Genius: "No one gets me... they don't appreciate what I have to offer."

And I came up with this one...

The Placater: "Oh, this is just temporary. If I keep banging my head against the wall... I'll either pass out or break through."

So, ask yourself, do any of those roles fit you? I know they have fit me... and quite well, thank you.

There's a novel called *The Line of Duty*, written by Michael Grant. In the book, a story is told about a fisherman who bought a new anchor for his boat.

As he's about to tie the anchor line, he falls overboard. Fighting for his life in 15 feet of water, he refuses to let go of that prized anchor. But eventually, he has to release the anchor so he can swim to the surface and survive.

One of the characters in the book uses that story as a metaphor for his life. He says,

"The job has been my anchor and I've held on to it for 23 years. I also don't let go, but I've run out of breath."

Well, show business was my anchor. But I was getting older. And though I was just as funny as I ever was (maybe funnier, he says modestly), the venues for earning a living and the lifestyle I wanted had dried up like a raisin in the sun.

And no amount of hoping, praying, or trying to wait out the blizzard was going to change the situation.

I had no choice but to let go of my anchor and commit to my reinvention. Once I did, a flood of prosperity rushed into my life. I then went on to success as a freelance advertising copywriter/marketing consultant/speaker. (Yes, a lot of titles... you should see my business cards!)

This isn't about me, though. It's about you. So what's your anchor? If you want to experience positive change, then you're going to have to let go of your anchor, recast yourself, and play the role that you were meant to play with your heart as your acting coach.

No doubt as you focus on rebooting your career you might get overwhelmed with what to do next. If so, then think of the old adage...

How do you eat an elephant?

Answer: one bite at a time. Do something every day to keep reaching your goals. Need to find a mentor or learn a new skill, and don't have the time? Then reread my time management chapter.

In my earlier chapter on having the mindset of a black belt, while study and reading about the art, I discovered that Elvis Presley was an eighth degree black belt in Kenpo Karate.

Second to singing, he loved and promoted the martial arts. On his guitar he had the Kenpo insignia plus the logo: T.C.B. This stood for Taking Care of Business.

Throughout your working life, you will discover that to reach the next plateau... to get what you want... you will always find yourself **taking care of your business**. Your own.

In conclusion, I want to share three stories of people, just like you, who took control of their work life and successfully rebooted their careers.

Allow me to introduce you to author, consultant, and speaker, Barry Maher www. barrymaher.com

Wrote 'The Book' on His Subject, Surprised His Bosses, and Reaped the Rewards!

"Peter, I reinvented myself completely not just with my co-workers but with my clients, my boss, my boss's boss and on up the line, simply by becoming 'the guy who wrote the book on it'— when I did in fact write what soon became the leading book on how to advertise in the Yellow Pages.

"(It wasn't that difficult. At the time there was only one other book on the subject.)

"Still the additional prestige that gave me in that industry continued for my entire time in the business and gained me recognition not just within my company but throughout the 14 billion dollar Yellow Pages industry.

"I have no idea how many people in my company had even read the book, but everyone up to including the CEO knew I'd written it. Many of my superiors were actually intimidated by that fact, especially when they'd find a big display ad for the book in the Wall Street Journal, or see me quoted in the New York Times, or a competitor's newsletter.

"It gave me far more authority than I ever would have had otherwise. And any statement, opinion, vision, or plan I offered was taken far more seriously.

"By the way, that book led to industry and then non-industry speaking engagements and consultations, a number of other books, and what became a very rewarding career outside the Yellow Pages industry."

Talent + Mentor + Saying 'Yes' to Everything = Success!

Maureen Nelson tells us how:

"In 2008, I worked as an employment specialist in a prison diversion program for young felons (mostly drug dealers). This was my first job after graduating with my M.A. in Career Development. For four months, I coached clients in job hunting and resume writing.

"They had spotty work histories and didn't think they could make it in the legal economy, but I drew them out to reveal their strengths. I had a background in editing, graphic design, and marketing, and I applied all three to the resumes I created.

"I used unusual layouts, graphics, quotes, and so on, to create beautiful documents that instilled confidence in the job seekers.

"My talent created some buzz — not just in my building, but all over the organization. Various employees, including managers and directors, started coming to me in 'stealth' mode for resume tune-ups.

"My talent caught the eye of the man who became my boss and mentor in the organization and he hired me to be on his team — still coaching on job hunting and resumes, but now working with a wider range of clients, including professionals.

"I only stayed with him five months before I left for my current employer, another non-profit organization in workforce development. "

The saga continues...

"In 2009, I was hired as a senior career counselor and again, I made a name for myself, not just in resume writing (my own resume has been published in Susan Ireland's 'The Complete Idiot's Guide to the Perfect Resume'), but in speaking and writing.

"I volunteered for everything: to go to speak at prison, to work job fairs, to write hand-outs, to teach classes. I've been interviewed on the radio a couple of times and featured in local newspapers.

"No job was too tough, too scary, too hard or too boring. I said 'yes' to everything, cheerfully.

"After a year, there was a re-org and expansion. My boss moved sideways and his position opened up. My name was put forth for the promotion and I got it.

"I'm now manager of adult career services, co-site manager of our career center, website content manager, sponsor of our professionals' job search group. I am also an instructor in a career development credentialing program that trains workforce development professionals in our local system.

"Only two years after entering this field, I've spoken at a national conference, won a national award and am working on a book/app proposal requested by the largest publisher in career development (JIST)."

From Sears Roebuck to Developing an Automated Process that Improved her Company's Efficiency!

April Williams of **www.CyberLifeTutors.com** reveals her reinvention journey.

"I was a stay at home mom in 1992 when I landed an interview at Sears, Roebuck & Co. At the time I did not know how to type, never used a computer, never worked at a Fortune 500 company. A friend of a friend knew of an opening and was confident I could translate the organizational, team building, process skills of mom-hood into the business world.

"I was hired and worked hard as to not let this contact down. There were 8 of us admins on the team supporting 8 buyers. When one of the admins left, I took on support for 2 buyers. They both told my boss that while I was pulling a double workload, they were getting better results than when they had their own dedicated staff.

"Over the next 6 months, I developed an automated process to reduce manual input from two days to two hours. As I found new ways to improve efficiencies, management saw I had a knack for this technology stuff. At the end of 1 year, I was team leader.

"Within 18 months with the company, I was promoted from data entry, to team leader, to IT desktop support for 300,000 workstations throughout the country. A year later, Q&A for a new customer support applications, still at Sears.

"My last role at Sears was IT manager for Sears.com outbound e-mails to customers and Sears.com website analytics with a multimillion dollar budget. It was a wild ride and I worked my butt off for 9 years with Sears.

"The evolution through these jobs required constantly learning new tools and technology. I was fortunate to get assistance getting my foot in the door. Once I was inside, it was all expecting the best from me and an assumption that I could do or learn anything I set my mind to. Turns out — I was right!"

Do you notice the common theme in the stories? These folks saw an opportunity and seized it.

I now invite you to write your own reinvention story (with the ending you want). In fact, I hope you'll use the strategies outlined in this book, and then shoot me an e-mail telling me all about it at **reinventnow@yahoo.com**

Remember: Wherever your career takes you, whether you stay at your present position, or find yourself on another path perhaps... it's up to you to do what is necessary to make it happen. In the words of Larry *The Cable Guy* — get 'er done!

Peter J. Fogel
www.reinventyourselfnow.com

For access to The Reinvention Guy's websites — please visit **www.peterfogel.com**. While there, sign up for Peter's e-zines and receive four **FREE** gifts.

7 Days to Effective Public Speaking E-course (Value $125) Access to this course and other public speaking products and services can be found at **www.publicspeaklikeapro.com**.

Humor This! E-zine www.fortune500comedy.com. Once you sign up, you'll receive the e-book: *Effective Workplace Humor To Use That'll Bring Your Company a Strong ROIL! (Return of Infectious Laughter)*. In this e-zine you'll learn public speaking, comedy writing techniques, and stress reduction strategies — plus how humor can improve the quality of your life.

Peter J. Fogel's Direct Response E-zine www.compellingcopynow.com You'll get the e-book: Marketing Secrets of the Masters! Peter delivers you high response copywriting and marketing strategies that you can use to help you prosper on-line or off, so your effective message will reach your targeted audience for maximum results!

Peter J. Fogel's Reinvent This! E-zine www.reinventyourselfnow.com. Sign up for Reinvent This! And receive *The Ultimate Reinvention Quiz* e-book. This site also has other products and reinvention tips that'll help you reach your goals faster than you ever thought possible!

For customized and inspiring presentation as well as how to book "*The Reinvention Guy*" at your next event, please contact Peter at **peterfogelspeaks@yahoo.com** or visit his website at **www.reinventyourselfnow.com**

Peter's Public Speaking and Reinvention Blogs can be found at www.peterfogel.com

Follow and connect with Peter at:

www.twitter.com/ReinventionGuy

www.facebook.com/Reinvention.Guy

RECOMMENDED READING

Adams, Douglas. *The Hitchhiker's Guide to the Galaxy*. Ballantine Books, September 27th, 1995.

Altier, William J. *The Thinking Man's Toolbox: Effective Processes for Problem Solving and Decision Making*. New York: Oxford University Press, 1999.

Boothman, Nicholas. *How to Make People Like You in 90 Seconds Or Less*. Workman Publishing Company, September 18, 2000.

Buzan, Barry, and Buzan, Tony. *Mind Map Book: How to Use Radiant Thinking to Maximize Your Brain's Untapped Potential*. Plume, March 1996.

Businessweek. *Reinventing Your Career: Following the 5 New Paths to Career Fulfillment*. New York, NY: McGraw-Hill, Inc., 1997.

Canfield, Jack. *The Success Principles: How to Get from Where You Are to Where You Want to Be*. New York, NY: HarperCollins Publishers, Inc., 2005.

Chandler, Steve. *17 Lies That Are Holding You Back and The truth That Will Set You Free*. Renaissance Books, September 15, 2001.

Covey, Steven R. *7 Habits of Highly Effective People*. Simon and Schuster, 1st Edition, September 15, 1990.

Diener, Marc. *Deal Power: 6 Foolproof Steps To Making Deals of Any Size*. Henry Holt & Company, Inc., January 1998.

Fisher, Marsh. *The Ideafisher: How to Land That Big Idea-And Other Secrets of Creativity in Business*. Petersons Guides, 2000.

Fisher, Roger, and Ury, Bill, and Patton, Bruce. *Getting To Yes: Negotiating Agreement Without Giving In*. Penguin USA, 2nd Edition, December 1991.

Gellerman, Saul. *Motivation in the Real World, The Fine Art of Getting Extra Effort from Everyone-Including Yourself*, Plume, September 1993.

Gladwell, Malcolm. *The Tipping Point: How Little things Can Make a Big Difference*. Back Bay Books, January 7, 2002.

Greene, Robert. *48 Laws of Power. Penguin*, September 2000.

Heller, Robert, and Hindle, Tim. *How to Delegate*. DK Publishing, January 1997.

Hochheiser, Robert M. *It's a Job, Not a Jail: How to Break Your Shackles When You Can't Afford to Quit*. New York, NY: Fireside, 1998.

LeBon, Paul, and Karam, Sara. *Escape From Voicemail Hell / Boost Your Productivity By Making Voicemail Work For You*. ParLeau Publishing, October 1999.

Lyles, Dick. *Winning Ways: 4 Secrets for Getting Results By Working Well With People*. Berkley Pub Group 1st Edition, December 4, 2001.

Pace, Diana. *The Career Fix-It Book: How to Make Your Job Work Better for You*. Naperville, IL: Sourcebooks, Inc., 2000.

Masterson, Michael. *Power and Persuasion, How to Command Success In Business and Your Personal Life*. John Wiley and Sons, 2005.

Pugh, Charles. *How to Jumpstart a Stalled Career*. Lincoln Wood, IL: VGM Career Horizons, 1994.

Russo, J. Edward, and Shoemaker, Paul J.H. *Decision Traps*. Doubleday. 1989.

Solovic, Susan Wilson. *Reinventing Your Career: Attain the Success You Desire & Deserve*. Franklin Lakes, NJ: Career Press, 2003.

Schulz, Larry Selling. *When You Hate to Sell: A Guide To Getting In Gear When You Fear Sales*. Schulz Sales and Marketing; (December 1, 1999)

The Leader of the Future. New York: The Drucker Foundation, 1996.

NOTES

1. Katherine Bicer." *Engineer Your Life*". Accessed Sept. 2, 2009. www.engineeryourlife.org/cms/6198.aspz.

2. Natasha Chilingerian."*The Winning Doc: queen-turned-physician*." American Press, June 20,2007

3. Brian Ness. Accessed Sept 2, 2009. http://mehs.d.umn.edu/.

INDEX

INDEX

INDEX